MARIA & NIKOS PSILAKIS

CRETAN COOKING

(The most delicious and wholesome cooking in Greece)

KARMANOR

Photography: **Nikos Psilakis**
Translation: **Maria - Teresa Xylouri**
Cover: **Roussetos Panaghiotakis**
Printing: **TYPOCRETA (KAZANAKIS BROS)**
Colour reproductions: **MORFI J.S.C.**
Bookbinding: **Z. Moudatsakis**

Lophos Semeli
715 00 Heraklion
Crete - Greece
Tel.-Fax: +30 81 261920
E-mail: npsilakis@otenet.gr

ISBN 960-7448-07-3

CRETAN COOKING

The cretan diet: a veritable miracle

"..The cretan has the lowest risk for coronary infarctions, the lowest mortality rates and prospects of the longest life in the western world."

Serge Renaud, "Le Régime Santé"

A few decades ago scientists from all over the world started showing an interest in the "mediterranean diet" and, more specifically, in the "miracle of the cretan nutrition". The research which was carried out on the island of Crete proved that its inhabitants enjoy exceptional longevity and excellent health, free from the diseases which torture people nowadays.

Today, the scientific research shows that the cretan diet saves lives and offers longevity. Cancer and heart diseases were rare as long as the Cretans followed their traditional nutritional habits. In his

Mortality rates after observation of fifteen years according to the Study of the seven countries

Per 1000	Coronary	Cancer	All causes
Finland	972	613	2169
U.S.A.	773	384	1575
Holland	636	781	1825
Italy	462	622	1874
Yougoslavia	242	394	1712
Corfu (Greece)	202	338	1317
Japan	136	623	1766
Crete	38	317	855

Adapted by A. Keys, 1986

Coronary mortality rate and general mortality (per 100.000)

	Study of seven countries (10 years)		International Health Organization (1987)	
	Coronary	All causes	Coronary	All causes
Finland	466	1390	386	1210
U.S.A.	424	961	263	1061
Holland	317	1134	224	1016
Italy	200	1092	148	1066
Yougoslavia	145	1021	137	1302
Corfu (Greece)	149	847	123	932
Japan	61	1200	53	837
Crete	9	627	7	564

book "Diététique: "Le Régime Santé", Serge Renaud presents some very interesting statistics taken from the famous comparative study of the "Seven Countries", which was carried out in 1960.

It was natural that, after the results of the research, it would be necessary to analyse the

reasons and try to explain the nutritional habits and the way of life of the Cretans which have remained intact for centuries. The famous American dietician A. Keys, pioneer of the research on nutrition, managed in 1957 to realize that which was going to be the inevitable conclusion of the scientific research after many years. Keys found out that: “the cretan peasants consume little meat and few milk products. On the contrary, how much oil, my God! It is the only fat they use in cooking. They add it or pour it abundantly on everything they serve”.

He was completely right! Today, as ever, olive oil is omnipresent in cretan cooking. It isn’t only the oil, though "The miracle of the cretan diet was also due to the pure natural products of the island and to the consumption of plentiful vegetables and pulses. In the cretan villages, till very recently, meat was not consumed more than once a week, and quite often once in 15 days. In coastal villages, the consumption of fish was a little more frequent. On the contrary the Cretans ate much bread - wheat or barley bread - vegetables, pulses, greens and fruits. They even used to cook meat with vegetables or pulses! Even on Easter day, a feast connected with meat-eating, the Cretans prepared their traditional lamb with artichokes, lettuce or with other vegetables of the season. For seven weeks before Easter they fasted the meat and the milk products, they rarely ate octopus and cuttlefish and once they ate fish (on 25th March, feast of the Annunciation).

On the contrary they ate snails very often which were abundant on the island. The Cretans love snails. Prepared with ground wheat or with vegetables they acquire an excellent taste. (The research of the authors of this book reveals that there are dozens of recipes based on snails).

Cretan cooking comprises a variety of over 100 edible vegetables, some of which are considered today to be particularly beneficial to our health, and such is the purslane. That plant has always been an integral part of the summer salad in Crete.

In the interesting book of Serge Renaud "Diététique: le régime santé" we read that:

"Among all the groups which were observed, either mediterranean or not, the group from Crete presented the lowest coronary mortality rate. After ten years of observation, that mortality rate went up by a hundred eighty four for ten thousands in the other mediterranean groups and only to nine in the cretan group, which represented a reduction of 95%. Certainly, the other mediterranean groups, the italian or the yougoslavian, had a coronary mortality much inferior to that of the group of Northern Europe or U.S.A., but the results of Crete were incredible!

The study made it apparent as well, after an observation of fifteen years, that Crete had generally the lowest mortality rate, irrelevant to the cause of death.

Today, the official statistics of the International Health Organization indicate that it is in Japan that we find the lowest mortality rate and consequently the best prospects for longevity. Yet, the table below shows that the total mortality rate of the two observed japanese groups is twice as high as that of the cretan group. Eventually we should know the official rate of mortality for the whole island of Crete. Despite all my efforts I haven't been able to find it. There is only that which refers generally to Greece. Yet, as is obvious, the mortality rate is almost double for Corfu compared to that of Crete..."

The authors of this book made great efforts to assemble almost all the recipes of the island, as well as all the historical information proving that cretan cooking hasn't changed through the centuries. The archaeological finds of the pre-historic period reveal that the minoan inhabitants of Crete ate bread, pulses, vegetables, fruits, snails and olives. Among the finds of the excavations there was a vessel containing shells of snails, conserved for more than 3500-4000 years, and another vessel of the same period with edible olives, conserved intact in the water of a well. Undoubtedly they were an offer to the "gods of the Underworld". In that period, just as today, olive oil was indispensable in the cretan nutrition.

Greek cooking reached its peak in the classic period. Those cooking traditions were preserved during the byzantine period and are kept alive today, while products not existant then (such as tomatoes) have been fully incorporated in the cretan nutrition and cooking. It isn't only the products and foods that are preserved in Crete nowadays, it is also the names of

the dishes. If an ancient Greek happened to participate in a meal in a cretan village he would feel quite comfortable; he would recognize a lot of the dishes and would know the names of many dishes which have remained the same for thousands of years.

The aim of the authors is to contribute to the preservation of the tastes and the dishes of the cretan cooking and to offer a good example of proper and wholesome nutrition to the contemporary man.

FOREWORD

On an international scale, there's much discussion in the scientific world about, and deep interest in, finding the ideal diet which will improve the health of human beings warding off illnesses. Ever since Antiquity, the traditional diet of the Cretans seems to be just such a one, including all the right ingredients. A comparative study among several developed countries, which began in 1960 on behalf of the seven countries, has a group of about 700 Cretan men from the countryside under medical observation, regularly checking the state of their health: so far this group has had the lowest percentage of deaths caused by heart attacks and different kinds of cancer. This study has also shown the Cretan population to be the longest living one: when, in 1991, thirty one years after the beginning of the study, the Social Health Sector of the University of Crete undertook the medical check-up of the members of the group, about 50% were found to be still alive as opposed to Finland where there wasn't a single survivor!

Cretans have been able to enjoy such perfect health and long life thanks to their diet. Until recently this diet was simple and wholesome: olive oil of course, which accounted for one third of the individual's daily need in energy, but mainly cereals, principally bread, pulses, vegetables and fruit and, to a lesser degree, cheese, milk, eggs, fish and a little red wine with every meal. Unfortunately, this diet has undergone some changes in the last decades, mainly among the younger generations, with most undesirable results for the general state of health of the population: a noticeable increase in early deaths caused by heart attacks and a widespread increase in malignant neoplasm. For this reason every effort which aims at restoring the traditional Cretan diet is of great importance: the editions KARMANOR, through their valuable efforts to put together traditional recipes from all over the island have acted as pioneers in this new field.

The recipes of traditional Cretan cooking published in this book explain the eating habits of the Cretans and the choices that have guided Cretan cooking up to the last decades. The first chapter of the book gives a detailed account of the simple and wholesome diet followed by Cretans in the past. Nowadays it is easy to choose from such an amount of recipes those which are best suited to our modern way of life. All the recipes which are prepared with innards and pork fat were prepared in the past only on special occasions, mainly during Christmas and Easter. Up to the beginning of the 60s Cretan peasants walked an average of 13 kilometres a day and today 70% of the Cretan population walks less than 2 kilometres daily! Which is why the modern inhabitants of the island don't need as many calories; therefore rich and fatty food is to be eaten very occasionally or even not at all.

Taking the conditions of modern life into account, we would recommend a return to the traditional Cretan eating habits, but with a noticeable decrease in the amount and frequency in the consumption of meat and other animal products. On the other hand, cereals (mainly bread), pulses, vegetables and fruit should represent 85% of our daily food.

The consumption of olive oil must be continued: it has been proven through several past and present studies that this excellent oil plays an all-important role in warding off illnesses and in preserving our good health. Contrary to other vegetable oils, olive oil is rich in monosaturated fatty acids which are resistant to oxidation and diminish the amount of LDL cholesterol without affecting the HDL cholesterol. This last one is a protection against atherosclerosis, whereas other vegetable oils are rich in polysaturated fatty acids and are sensitive to oxidation, producing LDL perioxides and oxides, which are particularly atherogenic. Moreover olive oil contains a vast amount of anti-oxidation factors like tokopheroles and hydroxyphenoles which, by bonding free toxic radicals, are a natural protection against atherosclerosis and different kinds of cancer. It is interesting to note that the composition of olive oil in fatty acids is similar to that of maternal milk.

Cretan traditional cooking makes use exclusively of olive oil, achieving excellent results both in taste and health conditions; it is therefore highly advisable not to replace it with any other vegetable oil, for these are not suitable in cooking and in frying. This is also the case of different sorts of margarine, a hydrogenation of vegetable oils and olive oil: margarine was completely unknown in traditional Greek cooking until a few decades ago. All these products contain fatty acids which are dangerous for one's health.

The Cretan recipes in this book, which have been arduously put together by the authors, give younger generations judicious advice and the opportunity to live on a perfect diet, avoiding the diets that derive from oriental religions (of the Guru type) which often have drastic and negative effects on one's health. A return to the traditional Cretan eating habits is a way of maintaining one's health and lessening the odds of falling victim to the plague of modern illnesses, such as heart attacks and cancer. Traditional Cretan cooking offers modern man a great food variety both in dishes and tastes, prepared on the basis of pure and natural products.

To conclude, the authors of the book make a specific note of the Cretan diet during the religious fasts of the Orthodox Church: indeed this regular vegetarianism, as established by our Orthodox Church, and in no way comparable to the strict, continuous and dangerous vegetarianism imposed by some food-faddists, seems to have excellent healthy results and is the object of a special research by the Social Health Sector of the University of Crete.

Antonis Kafatos
Professor of Preventive Medicine and Nutrition
University of Crete

Natural, traditional and local produce which give a clean taste to the food combined with the lovely customs of the local population are the hallmarks of traditional Cretan cooking. The roots of these traditions go very far back in time, straight to those remote centuries which have bequeathed to the Cretans their love of life and of good food.

The complex habits of the modern consumer have supplanted many typical traits of the traditional Cretan cooking and of the original tastes of the Cretans. For this reason the great effort on the part of the authors of this book to group old and forgotten recipes from all over Crete, and to publish them together with some that are still in use nowadays, has filled us with enthusiasm. It is our experience that traditional Cretan cooking appeals as much to the local population as to the foreigners who visit our island, offering them not only one of the most savoury and healthy cookery in the world, but also introducing them to a unique, century-old civilisation.

The Cretan Association of Hotel Directors strongly recommends this book as a means of implementing the traditional Cretan recipes that figure in it in the hotels all over the island: in this manner local tradition will provide us with precious elements, like the authenticity of tastes, the use of choice local products and the love and enjoyment of life.

for the Cretan Association of Hotel Directors
Kostas Komninos
President of the Association

An important gap in the selection, recording, documentation and propagation of our gastronomic wealth has now been filled through the inestimable contribution of this new book.
The Administrative Council, the members and friends of "Archestratos" (a non-profitable organization aiming at the preservation and propagation of the Greek gastronomic tradition) and, I believe, every Greek who has an interest in our cultural heritage, welcomes this important publication with respect: as a Cretan and as a friend of the authors, I feel both pride and pleasure.
Methodically and with great sensitivity, the authors give us a complete picture of the historical development of Cretan cooking from the Minoans, the Deipnosophists and the Byzantines up to the present time, pointing out the cultural unity of the Greek world, but at the same time emphasizing the particularities of each region.
This effort, long and laborious, is presented in a simple and legible way. The book includes introductory notes to each unit of recipes, folkloric background to the various dishes, frequent references to the nutritional and wholesome elements of the Cretan diet (particularly olives, olive-oil, greens and the whole range of herbs). The recipes have been given to the authors by the very people who put them into practice in their every day life. All this, and last but not least the rich illustration, are a precious contribution to the effort for the preservation and propagation of our Cretan gastronomic tradition.

Nikos Skoulas
Vice president of the center
"Archestratos"
ex - Minister of Tourism

CONTENTS

CRETAN COOKING

(Introductory note)

The development of Cretan cooking right up to the middle of the 20th century is typical of a way of cooking which relies basically on its own produce. The products of its agriculture, of its livestock and of its fishing, were until the last decades the basic source of nourishment in Cretan households and in local cooking.

Cretan cooking in its historical background finds its roots way back in ancient times. Although there aren't enough sources to give us a complete picture of the eating habits of the Cretans, we do know today that basically Cretan cooking hasn't changed since Minoan times: indeed there have been very few additions to the products which were familiar to the prehistoric inhabitants of the island. We know for a fact that Minoans used olive oil just as Cretans do today, that they stored their cereals and that they enriched their meals with the pure wine from the extensive Cretan vineyards and with the fish caught in the boundless seas that surround the island, and so on. We also know that many of the local products brought the Minoans, who were remarkable merchants, riches and power, enabling them to control business and navigation in all the Mediterranean and perhaps even beyond, along other sea routes, if we are to believe more daring scholars. It seems that most of the products for export were agricultural, though herbs as such were also very much in demand.

In classical years Cretan cooking doesn't seem to differ much from the cooking in the other regions of Greece. Our sources for this period are mainly Athenian, including however some (scant) information about Crete. Apparently cooking at that time had a general character all over Greece, though of course with some important local differences. Sweet and sour sauces, later on thought to be of French inspiration, have their origin in Greek Antiquity, as is the case with many specific tastes predominant nowadays in European cooking. A more profound study of eating habits in Ancient Greece would be of great interest as it would show the innovative contribution classical Greece has brought to the skill of cooking.

In the following years, Cretan cooking was enriched through contacts with other civilisations and the successive conquests of the island brought a mingling and interchange in the eating habits. It is a well-known fact today that the Roman ruling class appreciated Cretan culinary products, especially the wine (the Lyktios wine and the wine from Sitia were much sought after even at the imperial court).

Important innovations took place during the long period when Crete was part of the Byzantine Empire. It was the time when the famous Byzantine cooking was developing and Crete contributed greatly with her own cultural experience in the field. It's not by accident that most Byzantine dishes we find in literary texts are still to be found nowadays in Crete and with the same names. As a Byzantine "theme" (that is, province), Crete was outstanding in her contribution to this civilisation. And later on, after the breakdown of the Byzantine Empire and its conquest by the Ottomans (1453), Crete became the cultural capital of the orthodox world.

Many Byzantine scholars came to live in Chandax (known today as Heraklion) after 1453 bringing, together with all their belongings, the eating habits of Constantinople. During this period the island belonged to the Venetian Republic and the Venetian dignitaries, who settled down in the cities and in luxurious villas in the villages and brought their own eating habits to their new country. Different civilisations met and Crete became the melting pot for their different ways of cooking, which once assimilated and incorporated became part of the traditional Cretan cuisine. It is important to realise, though, that the traditional Cretan cooking formed the basis for all the tendencies and developments that followed.

The list of the products which are being exported from Crete during the Venetian period are of particular interest. Among them we find the wonderful Cretan wine (famous through the whole civilised world of the time), honey, olive oil, cheese and other items.

The Turkish occupation of the island (1669) had no influence whatsoever on the traditional Cretan cooking. The only "influence" which can be traced to this day are the Turkish names given to several dishes which, of course, existed long before the Ottomans. We must not be fooled today by these names. Cretan cooking is the direct and natural result of a civilisation which was developed by those people living permanently on Cretan land, tilling the soil and having at their disposal all the required supplies to shape their eating habits. On the other hand, the Ottoman Turks having lived for many centuries as nomads had got used to a more frugal diet, proper to people who were always on the move. Indeed if there is no vegetable garden, there can be no ways of cooking vegetables. But in any case Cretan traditional cooking couldn't possibly have been influenced by the new conquerors since there weren't any Turkish settlements on the island, which means that there was no mingling of the populations or cultural interchange. One must realise that the Cretan Turks who were living in Crete up to the beginning of the 20th century weren't of Turkish descent but belonged to that part of the population of the island who converted to Islam.

The Turkish domination of the island suspended all cultural activity and reduced the

Xenophon Spinthakis. One of the best known cooks in Heraklion in the beginning of the century. His family gladly gave the authors his famous recipes.

Cretan iconography: the "Last Supper" by Michael Damaskinos (16th century) and below an example from the church of Saint Andrew, Odigitria, Mesara.

SAINT EFROSYNOS, THE COOK.

Saint Efrosynos, the cook. Yet another example of cooking in Cretan iconography. Modern picture from the monastery Chrysopigi in Chania.

economy to its primitive form (subsistence farming). In the first years of the Turkish conquest, Crete lost its ascendancy in commerce and trade. All of this had an immediate effect on the development of cooking. Poverty and indigence forced the inhabitants of the island to look for easier and more accessible solutions to the problem of food. But even then the basis of Cretan cooking remained unchanged as is shown in the sophisticated dishes cooked for feasts and in the baking of a great variety of sacred breads, which are difficult to prepare requiring both knowledge and experience. When the Turkish domination ends in 1898, new eating habits are developing and one can observe reciprocal influences in the ways of cooking of different peoples. The Cretan cooking in towns was at that time very much under the influence of the customs in Asia Minor, due to the close contact that existed at that time between the inhabitants of the island and those of Asia Minor. On the other hand cooking in the villages retains its ancient properties even after the Union of Crete with the rest of Greece (1913).

In the next decades Cretan households continued to get their supplies from the local produce with the result that Cretan cookery became exclusively seasonal. Some products were prepared in the spring time, others during the summer and yet others in winter and all these products retained their full flavour bringing to the kitchen the fragrance of each season. Close contacts with Egypt enable the Cretans to get large supplies of spices which they widely use in their cooking. It is however important to remember that capers, origan and other such local products were never replaced but continue to be widely used, just as are native herbs for the preparation of wonderful tisanes.

The creative abilities of the local population are inseparably linked to the basic virtues still present in Cretan cooking. There are indeed very few plants and parts of the plant that are not used in cooking. The marrow plant not only gives us delicious zucchini, which can be served in a salad (boiled) or can be cooked in many different ways, either stuffed or fried (sfugatto), but at the same time the Cretan cook also uses the flowers of the plant (which are indeed very much prized on the island) or the tender shoots which are also cooked. In the same manner the leaves of the vine are eaten stuffed, while the tender shoots give an excellent, rather sour, taste; grape juice is an admirable natural sweetener, and of course raisins are used either for sweetmeals or in ordinary food (Cretan "omathies" and "tzoulamas" are famous dishes with raisins). And then too there is the olive tree, enhancing the beauty of extensive areas of the island, and offering priceless olive oil, the olives which can be eaten both raw and cooked. The oil always was and continues to be the basis of Cretan cooking. This outstanding product has been praised by scientists for its excellent

The hospitality of Abraham. We see here - for one more time in the cretobyzantine art- a frugal meal.

Red eggs are omnipresent at the Easter Sunday meal in all of Greece.

-A meal set against the deep blue of the Greek sea.

effects on one's health and general physical well-being and is always present in Cretan cooking, whether raw or cooked with a variety of foods. Nowhere else in the world is olive oil as much used as in Crete. And though certain travellers tried to link the vast consumption of olive oil with various illnesses which were endemic to the island in the past, modern scientific research on the contrary praises the Cretans for this habit, attributing almost miraculous properties to it: we were recently told that olive oil even cured cancer!

The use of animal fats was never widely used on the island, except at Christmas time when every household had a pig slaughtered

Weaving baskets in Crete (Photo by Koutoulakis)

and its meat used in the preparation of various dishes. But this was during a very short period and had no influence on the general diet.

Abundant greens, pulses, cereals and meat both from local livestock and game are to be found among other select products used in Cretan cooking. Cheese was also profusely used in stock-raising regions. In many of these, dairy products enrich the cooking giving the food a special taste. Assorted meatpies -meat pastries in Chania- provide an excellent example of cheese-made products.

Largely the same kind of cooking is to be found all through the island, though of course there are important varieties which set off the specific ways of life and household managing of each place. The "kallitsounia" and the "myzithropites", for example, are to be found everywhere on the island, yet the ones from Sitia, called "anevata", differ from the "agnopites" of Heraklion, from the "sarikopites" of Anoyia and from the "sfakianopites" in Sfakia. The use of the same (or very similar) ingredients result in different tastes...These changes are always due to the nature of each place and its people. The inhabitants of Sfakia don't go in much for sauces because the food had to be taken to the mountains where the stock-farmers lived and the conveyance of liquid food was difficult, whereas meatpies and other typical dishes from the mountain regions were easier to carry.

In this book local specialities are set off against the more general background of Cretan cooking. In many cases several different ways for preparing the same dishes are mentioned, after long and careful research in all the regions of the island... At the beginning of each chapter, an introductory note gives the historical and folkloric background and individual notes are given when a specific dish

Sheep on the mountain of Psiloritis.

has an historical or folkloric value.

In most cases the name of the person figures underneath the recipe he or she gave us. No names are given for the simple and common recipes to be found all over the island. In order to make the book easy to follow, the traditional Cretan recipes are presented in a common form and not as they were dictated to us. For the same reason we have put side by side the recipes presenting historical or folkloric interest, though they come from different sources. This means that the people who gave us the necessary instructions and dictated their recipes to us, often have nothing to do with more general information given before or after the recipes.

MEAT

If we are to believe archaeological findings, Minoans consumed a lot of meat. They bred oxen and other animals on their estates and there were a great many wild animals on the wooded mountains so that game was plentiful.

In Ancient Greece it was more a food for the well-off, specially the landowners who bred oxen, pigs, goats and sheep in their estates; though the poor also had meat, but not very often.

During the Venetian period (1211-1669), meat was rather expensive and the economy in rural Crete was a closed one. This closed economy in the rural areas imposed several ways and means of preparing and preserving meat so as to be able to consume it many months after the animal had been slaughtered. In medieval texts we find names given to the different kinds of preserved meat that are still familiar to the Cretans nowadays, specially in the countryside.

Among the many kinds, **"apochti"** is the least well-known today, although it was still being prepared during the second World War in the mountainous regions. It's a salted meat, dried in the sun or smoked.

"Apaki" (smoked meat) is a favourite dish in Crete. It's pork meat from the region of the kidneys. As for sausages they were prepared during Christmas time, when the pig was slaughtered. "Boldounia", stuffed with blood, and "salitsounia" were yet other kind of sausages.

Rissoles were called **"polpetes"** and were something like the meatballs of today, known as "keftes" which, contrary to what some believe, are not of Turkish origin.

"Patsas" is tripe, prepared then as today with the feet and stomach of the animal.

"Fouki" is known today as **foukaki** in many villages of Crete. It is pork meat specially cooked in the frying pan.

"Tseladia", known all over Crete as "tsiladia", is brawn.

"Omathies", still famous in Crete, was a special dish made of stuffed intestines. Formerly it used to be made with boiled blood, which explains the name: aimatiai-omatiai-omathies or amathies in some areas of Crete. (Aema means blood in Greek)

"Sgazeto" was like a stew, a kind of soup with meat and onions.

It is interesting to note that the Cretans of old preferred meat that had a sweet and sour taste, though there has been some doubt recently as to whether these tastes actually belonged to the old Cretan cooking: thus, many of these tastes have been put down to Turkish or French cookery. While it's a well known fact that the French adopted a great many cooking elements from Greece, the Turks had no cooking tradition until the conquest of Byzantium by the Ottomans. So it was Byzantine cooking that spread in the Ottoman Empire and gave birth to the Middle-East cookery, basically the Greek Middle-East cookery, from Constantinople, Smyrna and so on. The sweetish tastes of meat dishes were to be found in medieval Crete, just as they are today, long before the conquest of the island by the Turks.

A Cretan shepherd.

"Omathies", for example, were prepared with raisins which gave the dish a distinctive taste, like in the savoury and complex dish, found today in the region of Mesara (central Crete), which is called "tzoulamas".

Many of these names show a Venetian influence in Cretan cooking, and indeed the Venetians occupied Crete for more than 450 years. But Venetian cooking was of little consequence since Byzantine customs and tastes survived on the island for many centuries. Cretan cooking doesn't seem to have suffered any influence whatsoever during the following Turkish years (the Turkish occupation first set in 1669 and lasted till 1898). Indeed, there are no references to Turkish settlements in Crete. A conjunction of historical coincidences caused Cretan cooking to retain its Doric simplicity and at the same time the survival of many eating habits which had begun during the centuries immediately before. It is not in the least strange, for example, that the cooking of Sfakia should differ from that of Sitia: the former depends on livestock products, the latter on the produce of its agriculture.

In more recent years meat was not very often consumed by inhabitants of the plains, whereas it was more common among the mountain people who were stock-farmers. Yet in both cases the old ways of preparing the food and preserving the meat were kept. Until the sixties, while refrigerators were still unknown in Cretan villages, the ways of preserving meat were the same as of old. From what can be gathered, lamb and goat were the Cretans' favourite meat. The information we get from the Bohemian doctor Sieber (1818) as to a widespread illness called "podagra" (gout) on the island, may not be accidental: this was a time of closed economy, when every family produced its own agriculture and bred its own livestock.

The more complex meat dishes seem to have been more common in the western part of the island, where the local diet was enriched with all sorts of meatpies: here again the tight link with local production is evident. Raw materials are always to be found in the local agricultural and stock-raising supplies. In former years even spices were part of the local production. "Mousakas", a typical Greek dish, was unknown in rural Crete up to the thirties, but in the towns well-off families had been eating it at least since the end of the 19th century, as can be seen from the recipes in the notebooks of housewives of the time.

CHRISTMAS PORK

The slaughter of pigs is a national Greek custom with Roman origins: pigs were offered to placate the gods Chronos and Dimitra and invoke their help for good crops. The custom survived into the Christian era and is still to be found in most Cretan villages. Rural families slaughter the pig on Christmas Eve, which ends a period of long fasting: from the 15th of November to the 25th of December. During all this time the Cretan of old ate greens, which were abundant after the first rains, pulses, cereals and sometimes fish. In a way, it was a period for a natural wholesome diet, such as is recommended nowadays by dieticians. Christmas pork gave everyone the chance to eat lots of meat, after having refrained from eating any for so many days.

Each rural house had its own pig and pork was ever present at each Christmas meal. The most common dish on that day, "omathies" or "omaties", was of pre-Byzantine origin. In some regions the meat was cooked with "chondros" (ground wheat), and its innards in a pan, or else the meat was cooked on the coals of the open fire, always lit during the cold winter days.

The following day was a day of work for the rural family: they had to prepare "apakia", "syglina", and all other sausages and parts of the pork which were to be preserved for a few more weeks. The meat hanging over the hearth could possibly surprise a modern man from the town: not so a villager who knows that this is the way to preserve meat for weeks, sometimes months, to come.

"Tsiladia" (brawn).

Tsiladia

A head of pork
feet of pork
the peel of an orange
a cupful of orange or bitter orange juice
a cupful of lemon juice
half a cup of vinegar
salt, cumin, pepper, a little nutmeg

After cleaning thoroughly the head and the trotters, boil them in salted water until properly cooked. Remove the pot from the fire and when the meat is cold enough remove the bones. (The ears remain as such: they are one of the best parts of the "tsiladia"). Strain the broth (about 7 cupfuls), add the boneless meat chopped up and the juices (orange or bitter orange and lemon), the vinegar, the orange peel and the spices. When the mixture has boiled twice, remove it from the fire and let it cool off. Divide the brawn into several earthenware bowls (according to the quantity prepared), taking care that the liquid covers all the pieces and titbits. Leave in a cool place to set (nowadays in a refrigerator). With a spoon remove the fat from the surface, before serving.

Eleni Bitsakaki, Petrokefali.

***

"Tsiladia" or brawn, was prepared using the head and the feet of the pork on the day after Christmas. Left to set in an earthenware pot (the cold weather of the season helped), it was served on New Year's Day. It was an indispensable addition to the New Year's feast. Today this delicacy is prepared all the year round.

Omathies

A Christmas dish, widely known in the Byzantine world. Its origin, though, goes

back to Ancient Greece, where the blood of the animals was used in the preparation of certain dishes. The Byzantine "aimatiai" were made of the large intestine of the pork, the innards and the blood.

The blood was boiled until it set and then, with the boiled innards, it was stuffed into the intestine (in spite of the Church having strictly forbidden the use of blood in cooking). In Crete blood was also used in the preparation of another famous Medieval and Renaissance dish called "bouldouna". As the years went by the "aimatiai" went on being prepared as in Byzantine years, but without the blood of the pork. And they retained their name: "aimatiai, omatiai, omathies...

Today there are many different ways of preparing them in Crete but always stuffing the large intestine of the pork with innards. According to the way they've been prepared, they figure as a main dish or as dessert. Ground wheat or "chondros" was formerly part of the stuffing, but now rice is used.

A Cretan peasant
(photo by Anifandakis)

The fountain at Meronas, a village in Amari (1950)

Omathies with rice

(for 6-8 persons)
Intestines of pork and one pork liver
a little pork fat (though butter may also be used)
2 cups of rice
a handful of sugar
1 cup of raisins
1 cup of ground pistachios, walnuts or chestnuts
salt, pepper, cinnamon

Wash and bleach the intestines leaving them in a bowl with 3-4 lemons cut in slices and salt for 2-3 days.

Cut the liver into cubes and brown it in the fat or butter. Add water and when it boils add the rice and let it boil for 5 minutes. Add the other ingredients to the pot: raisins, nuts or pistachios, salt, pepper, cinnamon and sugar. Stir and then take the mixture from the fire and fill the intestines. (Be careful not to put too much mixture). Tie them up and let them boil in water for about an hour. Strain them and sprinkle them with sugar and cinnamon. (If desired, the intestines can be fried and browned in a little pork fat, when taken out of the water).

Irini G. Bitsakaki, Petrokefali, Mesara.

Omathies with orange peel

In the villages around Rethimnon, grated orange peel or citron peel is usually added, giving this dish a completely different flavour. As for the rest, omathies are prepared in the same way as above.

Eleni Simitzi, Rethimnon.

A typical cretan house (Historical Museum of Crete, Heraklion).

Other Christmas delicacies

Of old, when there were no refrigerators or deep-freezers, people found ingenious ways of preserving meat. This was particularly the case during the Christmas season, when the pig was slaughtered in every household. "Tsiladia", or brawn, "apakia", "syglina", sausages are some of the results of this inventiveness...

Apaki

"Apaki" is a smoked meat, known since Byzantine times and very common in Crete. It was made with the tender meat around the kidneys. A delicacy in Venetian times, it was to be found in most Cretan households.

The meat used for the "apaki" is cut in strips and left in a bowl with vinegar for one day. Then it is salted, peppered and hung over the fire-place. Several, freshly gathered Cretan aromatic herbs (origan, sage, laurel and others) are then burnt and the fire is covered with the ashes so as to make it smoke profusely. The meat is cooked in this fashion with the smoke and can be kept for many weeks.

OTHER DISHES WITH MEAT

«Tzoulamas»

(for 10 persons)

"Filo", a paper-thin pastry made with half a kilo of flour, 2 spoonfuls of olive oil, 1 glass of water and a little salt.

The **stuffing:** 1 lb. of pork or lamb liver
1 lb. of rice
1 handful of seedless raisins (sultanas)
1 handful of pistachios or almonds (in some regions chestnuts or walnuts are used)
1 cupful of butter
salt, pepper, cinnamon, nutmeg
1 cupful of sugar
1 cupful of chicken broth

Chop the liver, add salt and pepper and brown it in butter. Add water to boil the rice (2 cups of water for 1 of rice). A little before removing the pan from the fire, add the nuts and the raisins. Stir. Finally, add some sugar.

Prepare the "filo" and separate three sheets of paper-thin pastry. Butter a baking pan, open one sheet of pastry and sprinkle it with sugar and cinnamon. Spread half the stuffing and sprinkle again with cinnamon

"Tzoulamas".

and sugar. In the same manner put a second sheet of pastry and spread the second half of the stuffing covering it with a last sheet of pastry. Pour the butter and the chicken broth over the whole dish, sprinkling it once again with sugar and cinnamon.

Bake in a medium oven until the pastry turns golden.

Eleni Bitsakaki, Petrokefali, Mesara.

This is an essentially carnival dish, traditionally served in the region of Mesara. It is an old Cretan dish, not at all related to Turkish cookery, though its name changed under Turkish occupation. As we mentioned before, Cretan cooking has had Venetian influences but not Turkish ones, since there are no references to Turkish settlements on the island. (The so-called Cretan-Turks were Cretans who had converted to Islam.)

OFTO : AN ANCIENT CUSTOM

It's hardly surprising that the favourite way of cooking meat, even in our days, in Crete, is grilling it on charcoal. That is to say on the spit or "ofto" as it is known locally. The shepherds on the mountains of Madara and Psiloritis know of no other way (or at least use no other method) for cooking lamb and kid. The way they do it is most interesting, almost a ritual. The youngest shepherd clears an appropriate place discarding stones and bushes. He then digs a small hole in the earth in which he lights a fire, placing stones all around the hole to keep the spit in place.

- "Ofto" on charcoal.
- "Ofto" on the Psiloritis range.

These gestures recall Ancient Greece: Ancient Greeks dug exactly the same holes, which they called "vothros". There they made their offerings to the gods of the Underworld! So it is that ever since, or perhaps even earlier, lamb on the spit or "ofto" has been the Greeks' favourite meal. The shepherds up in Psiloritis don't wait till the coals are red, as they do in the rest of Greece, to cook their lamb. They skewered big chunks on the spit which has been prepared right then and there to allow it to cook at the temperature given off by the burning wood. They are, it must be said, very impatient. They are also impatient when they eat and they can hardly wait till the meat is cooked, eating it often almost raw or, let's say, half cooked. There's an explanation for this impatience: it goes back to the time of bondage. Meat on the spit requires fire and therefore smoke, and the smoke betrays the spot where the fire has been lit. The old time rebels, called "hainides", were always in a hurry, always on the run...

And what about the spit? It too has its origins in Ancient Greece. It looks like one of the spears the warriors of Ancient Greece used, not only in fighting, but to cook their own meat on the spit...

The shepherds of the Madara mountain followed another method when cooking meat on the spit: they dug a somewhat deeper hole, lit a fire and waited till it was reduced to only coals. The people from the region of Sfakia needn't fear the Turks in their inaccessible mountains and gorges, so they never cooked the meat on the flame of the burning wood, nor did they put stones around the hole.

All the inhabitants of the mountainous regions, specially those of Sfakia took great care in the cooking of wild animals, such as wild goats and chamois (a species of wild goat, unique in Crete, which at that time wasn't yet in danger of extinction). The connoisseurs of Sfakia never prepared wild goat on the spit because the meat of this wild and proud animal didn't taste good on the spit: it required the special attention of the women of Sfakia...

Lamb on the spit («ofto»)

An Easter meal, well established in all the Greek world. Some regions of the country, like Roumeli, claim the origin of this custom. In Crete it varies slightly from region to region. In most cases the lamb is not cooked in one piece, but in chunks and over coals in a shallow hole in the ground. In those regions where the lamb is cooked in one piece, it is cleaned and basted in lemon juice and oregano. Sometimes the "knisari" (the diaphragm) is twisted around it, and the greasy membrane melts into the meat as it cooks, giving it a more savoury taste.

A long time ago, the spit was a long, thin piece of wood about 2 meters long. Today there are special metal ones, some are even electric and turn automatically. Put the lamb on the spit, and tie it firmly, then turn the spit constantly over the coals (no flame) until the lamb is cooked. While cooking baste it with olive oil or butter. When chunks of meat come off the bone the meat is ready. The whole preparation of the Easter lamb is like a liturgy, a real feast with music (lyres), songs, dances, red eggs, special Easter cheese pies and a general feeling of happiness.

Chicken on the spit

(Kotopoulo sti souvla)

1 chicken
3 to 4 tbsps of olive oil
2 or 3 cloves of garlic
salt and pepper

Wash the chicken, rub it with salt and pepper, put the garlic in its belly and tie it up. Place it on the spit and grill it on charcoal. When it starts going brown, baste it with olive oil turning it regularly until it is cooked. It can also be grilled in the oven of an electric cooker.

At midnight on Holy Saturday the Cretans burn the effigy of Judas on a great big bonfire. The Easter celebrations begin and everybody sits down to enjoy the Easter meal.
Easter in a cretan village. The procession of the icons depicting the resurrection of Jesus Christ.

Lambriatiko

(for 8-10 persons)
1 head of lamb
1 kilo of lamb chops
1 kilo of rice
a little fat from the lamb (preferably the "knisari", that is the diaphragm of the animal)
skim of boiled milk (1-2 cupfuls)
salt

This is a special local Easter dish from the village of Kapetaniana in the region of the Asterousia mountains. A little after the celebration of the Resurrection of Christ, the three ovens in the village are opened and all the inhabitants take the earthenware pot in which they have prepared their Easter meal. This is eaten immediately after the midnight mass, and is the first meal with meat after a fast of many weeks. The food is usually put in the oven at nightfall, around 7 in the evening, and cooks slowly till midnight.

This dish is prepared in an earthenware pot. Clean the rice, salt it and place it in the pot, with the head of the lamb in the middle practically covered in rice. Put the lamb chops over it and some of the fat. Cover the surface with the skim of boiled milk. Put it in the oven and let it cook for well over three hours.

Giorgos Stamatakis, Kapetaniana, Asterousia.

Pilaff from the region of Sfakia

(Pilafi sfakiano)

(for 10 persons)

1 kilo of a 2-year old lamb and a chicken

1 kilo of rice

1 cup of «staka» (fresh goat's butter)

1 small glass of lemon juice

salt

Boil all the meat till cooked and strain. Measure out the stock and get it to boil. Measure the rice and cook it in the broth (1 cup of rice for 3 of broth). When the rice is half cooked, add the lemon juice. When it has cooked, take it off the fire, melt the butter and pour it over.

Evangelia Katsanevaki, Askyfou, Sfakia

Sikotaria

1 kilo of lamb liver
half a cupful of oil
1 onion
1 bunch of fresh dill
1 cupful of water
1 cupful of rice
salt, pepper
lamb suet
1 kilo yoghurt
4 eggs

Brown the onion and the liver in oil, add the dill, salt and pepper and the water; once it boils add the rice and bring to the boil again.

In a baking pan put some suet, then the mixture and cover again with suet.

Cook in a hot oven for half an hour. Take it out and pour over it the yoghurt beaten with the eggs.

Efi Varveraki, Heraklion.

Splinandero

1 kilo of spleen
small intestines
salt, lemon, pepper.

A delicacy to be found all over Crete.

Wash the intestines carefully and turn them inside-out. Wash again and clean them with lemons cut in half. Leave them a while with the lemon halves and then cut them in slices of about 10 to 15 cms long. Cut the spleen in strips, add salt and pepper and stuff them into the intestines. Tie the extremities with a thread and cook on the spit. In many parts of the island the spleen is boiled beforehand and then stuffed in the intestines: this way the "splinandero" is more tender.

Giorgos Kipreos, Heraklion.

"Kokoretsi" (Menuzes)

Kokoretsi (Menuzes)

All the innards ("sikotaria") are used for the stuffing. Cut the liver, the heart, the lungs and place them on long thin rods (spit) to make individual servings. Sprinkle with salt, pepper and origan; wind the intestines with great care starting at one end and finishing at the other, shaping a succession of 8s with the intestines. Do this several times and then wrap the intestines in parallel lines, making it firm. Cook in the oven with oil and lemon.

It is also possible to make a large amount of "kokoretsi", instead of the individual servings mentioned above.

Giorgos Kipreos, Heraklion.

Gardoumia

The stomach and intestines of a lamb
1 onion
salt and lemon
1 spoonful of flour
For the egg and lemon sauce:
2 lemons and 2 eggs

Gardoumia is yet another Easter dish in many parts of the island, simply because the Easter feast provides the ingredients: the intestines of the Easter lamb. In many villages in the region of Pediada, "gardoumia" is the first dish served after the midnight celebration of the Resurrection, on Easter Sunday.

Wash the stomach carefully, bleach it in boiling water and scrape it clean. Wash the intestines and turn them inside out with the help of a lean stick. Wash them once again and rub them with lemon juice, salt and flour. Cut the stomach into pieces the size of the palm of the hand and tie an intestine around each piece. Make a knot at the end (with the intestine), so it won't undo itself.

Grate the onion into the pot, put 3-4 cups of water and put in the "gardoumia". The food must cook until tender. Then take the pot off the fire and prepare the egg and lemon sauce.

Beat the eggs with the lemon and slowly add the broth from the pot; then pour this mixture back into the pot with the "gardoumia", beating constantly.

Loula Metaxa, Heraklion

Stomach with chick-peas.

Gardoumia with zucchini

(for 6 persons)
1 kilo "gardoumia"
1 lb. tomatoes
1 kilo zucchini
1 cupful of olive oil
1-2 onions
salt, pepper

The "gardoumia" are prepared as above, then browned in a pan with the onions and the olive oil. Add a little water and let it boil a couple of times. Add the zucchini and then the tomatoes skinned and chopped, the salt and pepper. Let the food cook gently on a low fire.

Katerina Koutsaki, Kali Limenes.

Meat with chickpeas

(Kreas me revithia)

This is a wedding dish in many parts of Crete. In the villages of Mesara it is cooked the day before the wedding and, with large quantities of red wine, is served to the guests. In the village of Anoyia, when weddings were on Sundays, this dish was prepared on the Thursday before, which was when the bridegroom's gifts ("kaniskia") were taken to the bride's house. On this occasion the bride's family served this meal, with lots of red wine.

Ingredients:
(for 6-8 persons)
1 kilo of meat (preferably pork)
1 lb. of chickpeas
a cup of oil
2 onions
one pound of skinned and chopped tomatoes
salt, pepper

Cut the meat in serving portions and brown the meat with the onion in a pot. Add the tomato, the pepper and the salt and let it simmer a while.

Strain the chickpeas (which have been soaking in water since the evening before) and put them in the pot with the rest of the ingredients. Add as much

"Gardoumia"

water as necessary and let it simmer until cooked.

Maria Kallergi-Xilouri, Anoyia

Stomach with chickpeas

(Kilia me revithia)

Follow the same instructions as in the above recipe. Instead of meat, use the stomach of a lamb or a goat and, if you wish, the intestines too. Both the stomach and the intestines must be carefully washed and chopped beforehand.

Loula Metaxa, Heraklion.

In many mountain villages of Crete (for example in Gonies in the province of Malevizi) stomach with chickpeas was the established wedding meal. Weddings were then held only on Sundays and the animals (lamb, kid, goat) were slaughtered between Friday afternoon and Saturday midday. The meat had to hang but the stomach and innards were more delicate. They had to be cleaned and washed immediately, otherwise they would spoil: the meagre country economy of Crete was too restricted to allow one to throw out spoiled meat so that the stomach and innards were washed and prepared and cooked with chickpeas on Saturday evening. On that day all the gifts ("kaniskia") were taken to the house of the bride and groom: offerings on the part of family and friends to contribute to the needs of the feast (meat, bread, wine and so on). The savoury dish with the stomach and chickpeas was then served, accompanied by large quantities of wine.

-Stomach with zucchini

Meat with fresh green beans

(Kreas me freska fasolakia)

(for 6 persons)
1 glass of olive oil
1 onion or 1 - 2 leeks
1 kilo of meat (either beef or pork)
1 kilo of green beans
1 lb. of ripe tomatoes
salt and pepper

Brown the onion or the leeks in the oil and then add the meat cut in portions, with a little water. Half way through, add the beans and the pulped tomatoes, salt and pepper and some water. Simmer till cooked.

-Veal stew.

Dried beans and meat

(Xera fasolia me kreas)

To be cooked like chickpeas and meat with the addition of two tbsps. of chopped parsley.

Traditional veal stew

(Stifado moscharaki)

(for 6 persons)
1 kilo of veal
1 cup of oil
1 kilo of onions
2 cloves of garlic
2-3 laurel leaves
2 glasses of red wine
salt, pepper and cumin.

Cut the meat into serving portions.

Put the oil, the onions roughly chopped and the laurel in the pot. Brown the meat in this, then add the garlic. When the meat is nicely browned, pour the wine to cover the meat. Add salt, pepper and cumin and let it cook very slowly.

Fotini Mattheaki, Neapoli,
Merambello.

Meat with zucchini

(Kreas me kolokythakia)

Cook as in the above recipe but instead of onion or leek use garlic and instead of beans, zucchini.

Veal with lemon juice

(Moschari lemonato)

(for 5-6 persons)
1 kilo of veal
1 small glass of white wine
salt, pepper
2 tablesps of flour

half a cup of lemon juice

Brown the meat with the onion and pour in the tumbler of wine. Add salt, pepper and water and simmer the meat very slowly until it has absorbed most of the liquid. Dissolve the flour in the lemon juice and add to the pot. Bring to the boil a couple of times and then turn off the fire.

Katerina Karkanaki, Heraklion.

Beef with potatoes (Vodino me patates)

1 kilo of beef
1 kilo and a half of potatoes
1 onion
1 cup of olive oil
half a kilo of tomatoes
1 spoonful of flour
salt, pepper

Brown the meat with the oil, the chopped onion and the flour. Add the chopped tomatoes, salt, pepper and a little water. Boil for about half an hour and then add the potatoes cut in slices. Boil for another 20 minutes and then take the pot off the fire. The dish is ready.

Marika Papamatheaki, Viannos

Meat Pasty (Kreatopita)

(for 8-10 persons)

The dough:
1 lb. of flour
1 cup of oil
1 tblsp.of concentrated tomato pulp diluted in water
a little salt

The stuffing:
1 kilo and a half of lean lamb
1 small cup of rice
1 lb. of assorted cheeses, diced
salt, pepper, cinnamon

1 grated tomato
half a cup of meat broth

Boil the meat and cut in serving portions. Mix it with the rice, the cheeses, the tomato, the broth. Add salt, pepper, cinnamon.

Prepare the dough and roll out two thick layers. Oil the baking tin and spread one layer. Place the stuffing on it and cover with the second layer. Add some oil on top and bake in a moderate oven.

Efi Varveraki, Heraklion.

Meatpie (Kreatotourta)

(for 8-10 persons)

The dough:
1 kilo of flour
30 grams of beer yeast
1 small glass of milk

Meatpie

2 eggs
2 glasses of meat broth
1 tablesp. of butter, salt

Stuffing:
1 kilo of lean meat (lamb or goat)
1 kilo of mizithra (a kind of soft white cheese)
3 tablesps. of "staka" (fresh goat's butter)
3 tablespoons of butter
salt, pepper, oregano
1 lemon

Cut the meat into serving portions . Add salt, pepper, oregano and lemon juice and leave it standing in a sieve for an hour.

Prepare the dough. First dissolve the yeast in warm milk, add some of the flour and let it rise. Then add the other ingredients and knead, adding not water but the broth. Roll out the dough and prepare two layers of pastry (half a centimetre thick). Butter, or oil the baking pan and spread the first layer of pastry. Put one third of the white cheese (mizithra), keeping it 2 cms. from the edge of the pastry. On top put half the meat and the second third of the cheese, and finally the second half of the meat and the last third of the cheese. Finally, spread the butter and the "staka". Cover with a layer of pastry, turning the sides of the first layer so as to close it tight. Dab with egg, sprinkle with sesame seeds and bake the meatpie in a medium oven for about two hours.

Evangelia Katsanevaki, Askyfou, Sfakia.

Small meat pasties

(Kimadopitakia)

The **dough:**
1 glass of water
1 glass of oil
2 eggs
1 glass of milk
1 teasp. of salt
1 teasp. of baking powder
flour (as much as needed)
The **stuffing:**
1 kilo of minced meat
1/2 cup of olive-oil
1 onion
salt, pepper and cinnamon

Prepare the dough. Brown the meat in the oil with the chopped onion, salt, pepper and cinnamon.

Roll out the dough and cut it out in round pieces. Put some meat on each piece and shape semi-circular pies. You can also make "sarikopites" by cutting the dough in long strips and rolling up the minced meat in them like a turban ("sariki", a turban, was also the local name given to the head-dress Cretan men used to wear-and some still do). Deep-fry them in very hot oil.

Katerina Karkanaki, Heraklion.

Meat balls with minced meat and potato

(Keftedes me kima ke patata)

This dish was commonly cooked in the village of Ayios Myronas, and maybe in other villages of the province of Malevizi as well.

Ingredients:
half a kilo of minced meat
1 kilo of potatoes
half a cup of olive oil
1-2 eggs
1 cup of grated cheese
1 cup of flour or rusk crumbs
salt, pepper

Cook the minced meat as usual with a little onion, but no tomato. Boil the potatoes, make a potato mash, add salt, a little pepper, the cheese, the eggs and the rusk crumbs or

A corner of a traditional cretan house. Museum "Lychnostatis", Chersonissos.

Cretans in a photo of 1921

Cooking pilaff from the region of Sfakia on the White Mountains

flour. Shape this mixture into small balls and dig a hole in the middle of each: insert some of the cooked meat, close the hole carefully with the potato mash and roll the "keftedes" in flour before deep-frying them in very hot oil.

Instead of using flour, the meat-cum-potato balls can be dipped in egg and in bread crumbs (or rusk).

Titika Miraki, Ayios Myronas, Malevizi

Roll of aubergines with minced meat

(Rolo melitzanes me kima)

(for 6-8 persons)
1 kilo of aubergines
1 lb. of minced meat
1 onion, salt, pepper
2 eggs
1 cup of bread crumbs

Cut the aubergines in long slices and fry them. Cook the minced meat with the onion and add salt and pepper. Spread the meat on the aubergines slices and roll them up. Dip the rolls in beaten egg and in bread crumbs. Deep-fry.

Anna Katsouloyiorgi, Heraklion.

Meat balls in a lemon and egg sauce

(Keftedes avgolemono)

(for 6-8 persons)
1 kilo of minced meat
1 cup of bread (without the crust)
2 onions
parsley, mint
1 cup of grated cheese
2 egg whites
salt, pepper
oil and flour for the frying

The sauce:
2 or 3 onions
a very small tumbler of vinegar
a small glass of milk
2 yokes
2 tbsps of butter
2 tbsps of flour

Prepare the mixture and shape the meat balls, roll them in flour and fry them lightly. Chop the onions and put them in a saucepan with a little water. As soon as they have absorbed the water, melt the butter and brown them, then pour the vinegar. Add a little more water, bring to the boil and put in the keftedes. Let them simmer.

Beat the yokes, add the milk, a little salt, 1 tbsp. of flour, 1 tbsp. of butter and a few tbsps of the stock. Add to the meat, stir and turn off the fire.

Mousakas

Nobody knows exactly when this savoury and delectable dish spread in Crete, though there are recipes for Mousakas since the end of the 19th century. It was a common dish among the town dwellers of Heraklion and Chania, and by the beginning of the 20th century it was also popular in larger villages close to the big towns. But for the families living in the country it proved a difficult dish to prepare, because it requires a lot of time and a great many cooking utensils. It's said that mousakas is the link between popular and sophisticated cooking. Although there aren't any sources to establish the date when this dish first appeared, mousakas figures in the oldest recipe notebooks of Crete: therefore it may be assumed that it exists on the island since at least the last quarter of the 19th. century.

Ingredients:
(for 8-10 persons)
Zucchini, aubergines, potatoes
1 kilo of minced meat
1 cup of oil
2 onions
a small glass of wine
1 or 2 tbsps of concentrated tomato pulp
3 eggs
1 cup of grated cheese
salt, pepper
1 cup of bread crumbs
For the **cream:**
8 tbsps of flour
4 tbsps of butter
2 litres of milk
2 eggs
salt, pepper, nutmeg

Mousakas

Brown the meat and onions in oil, pour the wine, add the tomato pulp dissolved in a little water and cook the meat. Then, stir in the eggs, the cheese and the bread crumbs.

Fry the zucchini, the aubergines, the potatoes, all cut in large slices. (These can also be baked with a little oil in the

A byzantine meal of roast pork (manuscript of 1362).

oven, to make a lighter mousakas; one can also use only aubergines or only zucchini).

Butter a baking pan, sprinkle it with bread crumbs and alternate a layer of potatoes with a layer of minced meat, a layer of aubergines and then a layer of meat, a layer of zucchini and again meat.

Prepare the cream: melt the butter; when very hot add the flour and stir till it colours. Add the milk and stir till it amalgamates. Finally, add the beaten eggs, the salt, the pepper and the nutmeg.
Pour the cream on the dish, sprinkle with cheese and cook the mousakas in the oven until it gets golden brown.

+Chrissi Prevelaki-Xiroudaki,
Rethimnon.

Cretan cannelloni
(Kritika kanellonia)

Cannelloni is a well-known Italian dish. In the region of Malevizi, people have been cooking cannelloni for a very long time, but it is not known if it is a survival from Venetian times, when Venetian and Cretan cookery influenced one another, or if it is a recipe of the 19th century.

Ingredients for the pancakes (20 to 25 pieces):
1 cup of flour
1 teasp. of salt
4 beaten eggs
2 cups of milk

- Cretan Canneloni

Beat the ingredients to a liquid mixture. Brush a pan with oil and pour in half a very small cupful of the mixture. Shake it so it covers all the bottom of the pan and put it on the fire to set. Then remove the pan from the fire and loosen the pancake with a toothpick, turn around very carefully with your fingers and cook it on the other side. Proceed in the same manner till the mixture is finished and leave the pancakes aside to cool.

Ingredients for the stuffing:
half a cup of olive oil
1 pound of minced meat
2 spring onions
1 egg
a handful of grated cheese
salt, pepper and a little nutmeg.

Brown the meat as usual with butter and the onions (but no tomatoes), place it in a bowl and add the egg, the cheese, salt and pepper. Prepare a thick cream, in a saucepan, with a tbsp. of butter (which must be heated till it burns), a tbsp. of flour and a small cup of milk.

Place some of the meat on the side of a pancake, smear some cream at both ends and roll up the pancake. Beat 2 eggs, dip each pancake and then roll it in bread crumbs. Fry on a moderate fire.

Titika Miraki, Ayios Myronas,
Malevizi

Giouvetsi meat with very small pasta

(for 6 persons)
1 kilo of meat (beef or mutton)
half a cup of oil
4 or 5 ripe tomatoes
1 lb. of very small pasta (like grains of rice)
salt and pepper
1 cup of grated cheese

Cut the meat into small portions, wash it and put it in a tin or earthenware casserole (you can also divide it into several small earthenware dishes). Pour the pulped tomatoes over the meat, add salt and pepper. Then add the oil with a glass of water and bake the meat in a moderate oven. About a quarter of an hour before it is cooked, add the pasta with 4 glasses of hot water, mixing it well with the tomato and adding some salt. Serve sprinkled with grated cheese.

Lamb (or kid) with fennel leaves

(Arni me maratha)

(for 5 persons)
1 kilo meat
1 kilo fennel leaves
2 lemons
1 cup of olive oil
salt, pepper.

Brown the meat in the oil. Add the chopped fennel leaves and boil for about an hour. Finally add the lemon juice, salt and pepper. Bring once more to the boil: the dish is ready.

Giorgos Stamatakis, Kapetaniana, Asterousia

Meat with small pasta: "Giouvetsi"

Lamb (or kid) with ochra
(Arni me bamies)

(for 6 persons)
1 kilo of lamb (or kid)
1 kilo of ochra
1 lb. of tomatoes
1 cup of olive oil
1 onion
a small cup of vinegar
salt and pepper

Clean the ochra, pour some vinegar on them and let them stand. Brown the meat in the pot with the oil and the chopped onion. Chop and skin the tomatoes, add to the meat. Simmer till the meat is half cooked. Then add the ochra, salt, pepper, a little water if needed, and simmer till cooked.

Eupraxia Psilaki, Kastamonitsa, Heraklion.

Lamb (or kid) in an egg and lemon sauce
(Arni avgolemono)

(for 5 persons)
1 kilo of meat
2 or 3 spring onions
1 small bunch of dill
1 cup of oil
2 eggs, 2 lemons
salt, pepper

Brown the meat in the olive oil and add the chopped onion and dill, the salt and pepper, and as much water as needed.

Once the meat has cooked, prepare the egg and lemon sauce beating the lemon juice with the eggs and adding a few spoonfuls of the broth. Remove the pot from the fire to keep the sauce from curdling, pour it over the meat and stir.

Eleni Simitzi, Rethimnon.

Meat with ochra

Lamb or kid with artichokes

(Arni me anginares)

Cook the meat as above, but half way through put in the hearts of 1 kilo of artichokes (cut cross-wise, but leaving them whole). Let the food cook and at the end pour in the egg and lemon sauce.

Manolis Stratakis, Heraklion.

Lamb or kid with lettuce

(Arni me marouli)

The same as above but replace the artichokes with 2 or 3 heads of lettuce.

Lamb or kid with chicories or spinach

(Arni me radikia or spanaki)

Follow the same instructions as above.
Eleni Simitzi, Rethimnon.

Goat in tomato sauce

(Aega me tomata)

(for 6 persons)
1 kilo and a half of meat
1 cup of oil
1 small onion
1 kilo of ripe tomatoes
salt, pepper.

A traditional autumn dish to be found all over Crete.

Brown the meat and the onion in the oil and, half way through, add the skinned and chopped tomatoes, the salt and pepper and some water, if needed. Simmer till cooked.

Stefania Papadaki, Axos, Milopotamos.

Goat cooked with tomato sauce and potatoes

(Aega me patates)

Cook the meat as in the above recipe and, with the tomaoes,add 1 kilo of potatoes. Simmer.

Giorgos Kipreos, Heraklion.

Pork with celery

(Chirino me selino)

(for 6-8 persons)
1 kilo and a half of boneless pork
2 kilos of celery
2 onions
1 glass of oil

Pork and celery

half a small glass of lemon juice

salt and pepper

This is the traditional dish served on the feast of Ayios Dimitris in the village of Platanias, in Chania. All the housewives prepare pork with celery on the 26th of October, nameday of the Saint. Saint Dimitris is the patron saint of Platanias.

Boil the celery in water for 5 minutes and then strain it.

Cut the meat in serving portions and brown it with the onions in oil. Add some water and let the pork cook for about three quarters of an hour. Add the celery, the salt and pepper and continue cooking on a low fire. Don't stir the food with a spoon: simply gently shake the whole pot so as to avoid burning the meat. When the water has been absorbed and the meat is cooked, add the lemon juice.

(Wild celery can also be used)

Maria Koulizaki, Platanias, Chania.

Pork with ground wheat

(Chirino me chondro)

(for 6 persons)
1 kilo of pork
1 cup of "chondros"
2 eggs and 2 lemons
salt.

Place the meat in the pot, salt it, cover it with water and let it boil to remove the froth on the surface. Then let it simmer. When it has cooked, take the meat out and strain the stock. Clean the pot, add more water and bring the broth to the boil; add the "chondros" and the salt. When the ground wheat is cooked, take the pot from the fire and prepare the egg and lemon sauce: beat the white and the yokes of the eggs separately, add the lemon juice, slowly add some of the broth . Finally pour the sauce into the pot stirring all the time and the soup is ready. (This dish can also be eaten without the egg and lemon sauce)

Maria Koulizaki, Platanias, Chania.

"Chondros" is roughly ground wheat, so that it won't become flour. See further on the chapter on pasta.

Pork wine snack

(Chirinos mezes)

1 kilo of pork
2 cloves of garlic
1 lb. of skinned and chopped tomatoes
1 tumbler of wine
salt, pepper and cumin

Brown the garlic in oil. Add the tomatoes and simmer. Add the wine, the salt, the pepper, the cumin and the meat cut in very small pieces. Simmer until cooked.

Giorgos Kipreos, Heraklion.

Rabbit «xekafkalota»

(for 6 persons)
1 small rabbit
olive oil for frying
a little flour
1 small glass of wine
salt, pepper.

Cut the rabbit in serving portions and leave it to marinade half an hour in the wine. Strain it, add salt and pepper and brown it in hot oil. Then pour the wine and let it bubble; let it cook a little longer.

(If the rabbit pieces aren't flat, beat them lightly before cooking.)

Loula Metaxa, Heraklion.

Rabbit stuffed with «mizithra»*

(Kouneli gemisto me mizithra)

(for 6-8 persons)
1 medium sized rabbit
1 kilo "mizithra"
2 tbsps. of butter
origan, salt, pepper.

Anoint the rabbit with the spices and the butter and stuff it with "mizithra". Then tie it up, or sew it with thread, wrap it up in grease proof paper and tie it again. Braise at a low temperature.

Argiro Manousaki, Boulgaro, Kisamos.

**a soft white cheese*

Rabbit with yoghurt

(Kouneli me yiaourti)

(for 6 persons)
1 rabbit
2 lemons
1 cup of oil
2 or 3 tbsps of butter

Meat with yoghurt

1 lb of yoghurt
4 eggs
salt, pepper

Wash the rabbit and marinade it for several hours in the juice of the lemons. Then place it in a baking pan, add salt and pepper, pour the oil, the butter and some water over it and roast it. When cooked, take it out of the oven, mix the yoghurt with the beaten eggs and 2 or 3 tbsps of water and pour this mixture over the rabbit. Put the dish back into the oven until the sauce has thickened.

Niki Giannikaki, Therissos, Kidonia.

Rabbit stew

(Kouneli stifado)

(for 6 persons)
1 rabbit
1 lb. of onions
2 or 3 cloves of garlic
1 cup of oil
1 small tumbler of red wine
1 lb. of ripe tomatoes
half a tbsp. of concentrated tomato pulp
2 cinnamon sticks and 5 or 6 cloves
2 or 3 laurel leaves, salt, pepper, cumin

Cut the rabbit into serving portions and brown it in the oil. Pour in the wine and let it bubble.

Then add the roughly chopped onions and when they are half cooked add the chopped tomatoes and the concentrate diluted in water, the garlic, the laurel leaves, the cinnamon, the cloves, the salt and pepper, the cumin and a little water. Cook for about one hour.

Titika Saklabani, Heraklion.

Hare in wine

(Lagos krasatos)

(for 6 persons)
1 hare
2 tumblers of red wine
2 or 3 onions
2 cloves of garlic
3 or 4 laurel leaves
2 or 3 cloves
salt, pepper
2 tbsps of flour, 1 cup of oil

Overnight marinade the hare, which has been cut in several pieces, in the wine, the onions, the garlic, the laurel leaves, the cloves and the pepper. Next day brown it in oil. Add the flour, stir and add the liquid in which the hare was marinating. Add some salt and simmer till cooked.

Menelaos Arkalakis, Listaros, Pirgiotissa.

Hare stew

(Lagos stifado)

(for 6 persons)
1 hare
1 cup of oil
1 kilo onions
1 tumbler of wine
1 tbsp. of concentrated tomato pulp
3 or 4 laurel leaves
salt, pepper, cumin

- *Meat stew*

1 tbsp. vinegar

Cut the hare in pieces, place them in a pot with the oil, the salt and the wine. Let the food simmer a little and then add the roughly chopped onions, the concentrate diluted in water, the pepper, the cumin and the laurel leaves. Simmer. Shortly before it has cooked, add the vinegar.

Manolis Stratakis, Lasithi - Heraklion.

Chicken pilaff

(Kotopoulo pilafi)

(for 6 persons)
1 chicken
1 lb. of rice
salt, lemon
grated cheese

Cut the chicken into large portions and place in a pot with salted water. Bring to the boil, remove the froth and let it cook. Then place it on a dish. Measure out the broth, bring to the boil, and add the cleaned rice, counting 1 cup of rice for 2 and a half of broth. Stir a couple of times and turn off the fire. Add a little lemon to the pilaff, and if you like, a little "staka" (fresh goat's butter), or else sprinkle with lots of cheese and cook it in the oven for 5 minutes.

Toula Kalaitzaki, Heraklion.

Chicken with parsley

(Kotopoulo me maintano)

(for 6 persons)
1 chicken
1 kilo parsley
1 cup of oil
salt
2 lemons
1 egg

Wash the chicken and cut it into portions. Put it in a pot to brown in the oil and then add the parsley. Add 1 cup of water and some salt: let it simmer. When it has cooked, prepare the egg and lemon sauce: beat the egg, add the lemon, and some of the broth from the pot; pour this sauce on the chicken and remove from the fire.

Kostas Petrakis, Heraklion.

Chicken in the oven

(Kotopoulo sto fourno, pane)

(for 6 persons)
1 chicken, 2 cups of bread crumbs
1 glass of milk, salt, pepper

Cut the meat in large portions. Salt and pepper each portion, dip it in milk, then in bread crumbs. Place a sheet of grease proof paper dabbed with oil or olive oil: on it place the pieces of chicken and roast without turning the portions around.

Titika Miraki, Ayios Myronas, Malevizi

Chicken with peas

(for 6 persons)
1 chicken, 1 cup of olive oil
1 small cup of lemon juice
1 kilo of peas, salt, pepper.

Cut the chicken in large pieces, salt them, place them in a baking pan with the skin underneath and pour a cup of olive oil or of melted butter over them. Cover the pan with some sort of lid (today we can use aluminium paper) and place it in the oven at a temperature of 200 degrees. Half an hour later uncover the pan, turn the portions and baste them with lemon juice. When the meat is almost cooked, add the peas, in the middle of the pan, adding a little water if needed. Cook for another 15 minutes.

Titika Miraki, Ayios Myronas, Malevizi

Chicken in the oven with cheese

(for 6 persons)
1 chicken, 1 lb. of cheese (preferably "graviera")
butter, salt

Cut the fowl in serving portions and boil it. When it has cooked, let it cool off and then remove the bones. Butter a pan, put the chicken pieces and place a slice of cheese ("graviera") on each piece. Leave in the oven until the cheese melts.

Chrisoula Koulizaki, Platanias, Chania.

Chicken with oregano

(for 6 persons)
1 chicken
1 cup of olive oil and some frying oil
1 onion
1 small cup of lemon juice
1 tbsp. of oregano, salt

Cut the fowl in serving portions and leave them for four hours in salted water. Then take off the skin, which, because of the salted water, will come off easily. Brown the portions in oil. Then put the chicken in a pot and boil it with the oil, the quartered onion, the lemon, the oregano and enough water to cover the pieces: when the water has been absorbed, the chicken is ready.

Marika Koulizaki, Platanias, Chania.

Chicken in tomato sauce

(Kotopoulo kokinisto)

(for 6 persons)
1 chicken
1 cup of oil
1 onion
1 kilo of ripe tomatoes, salt, pepper

Brown the chicken, cut in pieces, in the oil with the onion.

Then add the chopped and skinned tomatoes, salt, pepper and a little water. Simmer.

Chicken with ochra

(for 6 persons)
1 chicken
1 cup of olive oil
1 onion
1 kilo of ripe tomatoes
salt, pepper.

Brown the chicken in the oil with the onion and add the skinned and chopped tomatoes, salt and pepper and a little water. When cooked, remove the chicken portions with a ladle. In the meantime, prepare the ochra: wash them, clean them and pour a cup of lemon juice or the juice of sour grapes over them ("angourida"). Let them stand for an hour or two before adding them to the chicken broth. Once cooked, mix with the chicken.

Titika Saklabani, Heraklion.

P. 65: *-Minoan mural depicting a fisherman (Santorini)*

- Fishermen cleaning their nets
-Baked fish

FISH

Fish was naturally to be found among the sea-side population of Crete, but was not at all common inland, specially in the more remote villages. Rock fish, octopus and cuttlefish were among the favourites. "Kakavia" (a fish soup) was one of the most inexpensive and common dishes on the coast: it is made with a great variety of fish, boiled all together. But the other products, common to all Cretan households also had to be used: this inspired Cretan housewives and they concocted unusual dishes, mixing several different tastes. Fish with ochra is an example, a dish to be found in Sitia, Malia and the coastal villages of Rethimnon.

Preserved fish (salted whiting -the Mediterranean version of cod-, dried cuttlefish) were quite common of old in Crete. Cretan housewives found many and interesting recipes to include them in their cooking.

FISH SOUP

It is the most famous and common dish of the fishermen on the Greek islands. It is a very delicious and wholesome dish, particularly popular among the people of the coastal regions of Crete. At Mochlos, the picturesque sea-side settlement of the province of Sitia, fish soup was the food cooked on Whit Monday. On that day the people of the nearby villages went downhill to the seaside and celebrated all together with good wine and violins or lyres. They often cooked plenty of fish soup in big dixies using the best fish caught by the fishermen on that day.

In many coastal villages of Crete, where Saint Nikolaos, protector of the seamen, is worshipped as their patron saint, fish soup is the main dish on 6th December, the day of the saint's feast. At Agios Nikolaos, the beautiful tourist town of Eastern Crete, the fishermen used to offer people fish soup on 6th December each year.

Fish with ochra

Fish with ochra

(Psari me bamies)

(for 6 persons)

1 kilo of fish (preferably sea-bream or blackfish)

1 kilo of ochra

1 cup of oil

1 lb. of tomatoes

1 or 2 onions

a little lemon juice or vinegar

salt, pepper

Clean the fish. Wash the ochra, clean them and let them stand in a bowl with salt and vinegar (this is so they won't dissolve in the cooking).

Brown the onion in a pot and add the ochra, the tomatoes, salt and pepper and simmer till half cooked. Remove half the ochra, place the fish on the ochra in the pot and add the other half. Bring to the boil and cook.

+Petros Charamis, Heraklion.

Fish in the oven

(Psari sto fourno plaki)

(for 5 persons)
1 kilo of fish
1 cup oil
1 lb. of tomatoes
a bunch of parsley
2 cloves of garlic
1 cup of bread crumbs
salt
pepper
the juice of one lemon

Chop the parsley and garlic small and mix with salt, pepper and bread crumbs. Chop half the tomatoes and place them in a baking pan. Place the fish on top and sprinkle with the above mixture of parsley, garlic and so on. Then add the rest of the tomatoes, also chopped small, pour the oil and the lemon juice on the whole dish. Cook in a medium oven.

Eleni Daouraki, Sitia.

Fish in the oven with oil and oregano

(Psari sto fourno ladorigani)

(for 6 persons)
1 kilo fish
1 kilo of potatoes
a cup and a half of oil
the juice of 2 lemons
salt
pepper and oregano

Clean and cut the fish in slices. Place it in a pan with the sliced potatoes all around it. Sprinkle with salt, pepper and oregano and pour the oil, the lemon juice and a little water over it. Cook it in the oven at a moderate heat for about an hour.

M. Kyriakakis, Chania.

The little fisherman of Chiona in Sitia

Grouper aspic

(Sfirida pichti)

Fry and debone the fish. According to the amount of liquid, add the juice of bitter oranges or lemons, salt, pepper and cumin. Place the fish back in the liquid: bring to the boil. Once it has cooked, place it on a suitable plate and leave it to set.

Spiros Charamis, Heraklion.

Fried red mullet

(Barbounia tiganita)

1 kilo of red mullet
1 cup of olive oil
flour
salt

A common dish on the islands and the coast of Crete. Instead of red mullet, one can use other fish. Salt the fish, roll it in flour and deep-fry in olive oil until both sides are brown. Serve in a large dish with some parsley. Lemon juice is to be used sparingly as it softens the light crust obtained through frying the fish.

Marinated red mullet

(Barbounia marinata)

Fry the fish as above. In the meantime prepare the following sauce: heat a cup of olive oil, add some flour, stir, add a tumbler of white dry wine, a little vinegar, salt and pepper, and a small bunch of rosemary. Pour this sauce over the fried fish.

Fish with zucchini

Fish with zucchini

(Psari me kolokythia)

(for 6 persons)
1 kilo fish (preferably fillet)
1 kilo zucchini
1 lb. of tomatoes
1 cup oil
1 onion
salt, pepper
Wash, slice open and salt the zucchini.

Clean and salt the fish. Gently fry the zucchini. Place the fish in the middle of a pan with oil and the zucchini all around it. Cook the onion and the crushed tomatoes in the oil in which the zucchini were fried and pour this sauce over the fish and the zucchini. Add pepper, a little water and cook in a medium oven.

Eleni Simitzi, Rethimnon

Marinated red mullet. Above, branches of rosemary used in the preparation of this dish.

Grilled fish

Red bream or red mullet on the grill

(Lithrinia - barbounia sti shara)

1 kilo of large sized fish (5 to 6 fish for a kilo)
1 cup olive oil
2 lemons
a small bunch of finely chopped parsley
salt
oregano

Wash and clean the fish; place them on the grill. Let them brown gently, turning and basting them with oil at regular intervals. Serve in a large dish with slices of lemon and parsley. Sprinkle with oregano. Prepare some oil and lemon sauce which you can pour on the fish or serve separately so that each one can serve himself. Fishermen, however, prefer eating fish which have a strong taste, as is the case of the red mullet, without parsley or oregano, or any other trimmings.

Gilt-head bream on the grill

(Tsipoures sta karvouna)

This fish has more fat than red mullet, therefore grill it using less oil to baste it with.

Boiled fish

Poached fish - fish soup with vegetables

(Psari vrasto - psarosoupa me lachanika)

(for 6-7 persons)

1 or 2 large fish (sea-bream, dentex, grouper, gurnard (piper), blackfish etc.)
2 or 3 onions
2 tomatoes
a bunch of celery
5 or 6 carrots
1 lb. of zucchini
1 lb. of potatoes
half a cup of oil
a cup of rice
2 eggs
2 lemons
salt and pepper

Put the potatoes and the carrots cut in large pieces, the zucchini, the tomatoes and the onions sliced open and the celery into a pot with water. When all this starts boiling, add some salt and the oil. When the vegetables are half cooked, add the cleaned fish. Once the fish is cooked, take all the ingredients out and place them in a large dish with the fish in the middle and the different vegetables all around it.

Now strain the fish stock and return it to the pot; when it boils, put in the rice and let it cook before taking the pot off the fire. The soup can be served simply with lemon, or with an egg and lemon sauce, with 2 eggs and the juice of 2 lemons. Beat the eggs, add the lemon juice and finally, slowly, add a few ladlefuls from the soup, stirring constantly. Pour the sauce back into the pot: the soup is ready.

Maria Bitsakaki, Heraklion.

-Monkfish with green peppers
- Octopus stew

Monkfish with green peppers

(Lagopsaro me piperies)

(for 5 persons)
1 kilo fish
1 kilo green peppers
1 cup olive oil
salt and pepper

Cut the green peppers in round slices and place half of them in a pan. On top, put the fish with salt and pepper and, over it, the rest of the green peppers. Pour the oil on that and cook in a moderate oven.

Antonis Kouroupis, Heraklion.

Octopus stew

(Chtapodi stifado)

(for 5 persons)
1 kilo octopus
1 cup of oil
1 kilo of onions

- Fried squid
-Bream on charcoal

1 small tumbler of vinegar
2 or 3 cloves of garlic
3 or 4 laurel leaves, salt, pepper

Brown the onions in the oil. Add the octopus, cut in small pieces. Let it simmer on a low flame; towards the end, add the garlic, the vinegar, the laurel leaves, the pepper, a little salt and a little water, if needed, to let it cook a little longer.

Chariklia Charami, Plakalona, Kisamos.

Red mullet with artichokes

(Barbounia me anginares)

Put the artichokes in a pot with a cup of oil, salt, pepper and lemon. Add some water and the fish and cook till the fish is ready.

Dimitris Charamis, Heraklion.

Swordfish on the spit

(Xifias souvlaki)

Dice the swordfish. Dice, too, 2 firm tomatoes, 2 large green peppers and 2 onions. Mix with oil, salt and pepper. Skewer the fish and the vegetables alternatively. Grill gently.

Antonis Englezakis, Heraklion.

Monkfish on the spit

(Peskandritsa souvlaki)

The same as above (swordfish on the spit)

Antonis Englezakis, Heraklion.

Tuna fish with tomato

Tuna fish and tomato

(Tonos me tomata)

(for 6 persons)
1 kilo of fresh tuna fish
1 cup of olive oil
1 or 2 onions
1 or 2 cloves of garlic
4 or 5 ripe tomatoes
salt, pepper

Cut the fish in slices and wash it. (If you like, you can bleach it first in a glass of vinegar). Brown the onion and the garlic in the oil, then add the tuna slices turning them over several times. Add the pulped tomatoes and a glass of water, salt and pepper: let the tuna simmer in this sauce for about half an hour.

Antonis Englezakis, Heraklion.

Fried picarel - fried atherine (silverside)

Small fish are usually fried in hot oil. If the fish is tiny, don't try cleaning it: simply roll it in flour and deep-fry. In the Cretan villages of the coast, the tiny fish are often bunched up by their tails after rolling them in flour (flour helps keep them together); they are then all fried in groups and are easier to serve.

- Octopus
-Octopus in wine
-Small fry

Kakavia

(Fish soup)

(for 6 persons)
1 kilo and a half of big fish
1 lb. of smaller fish
1 or 2 tomatoes
a bunch of parsley
a bunch of celery
2 onions
1 cup olive oil
salt
lemon juice

Bring water to the boil and add the oil, the tomatoes sliced open, the onion, the parsley, the celery, the salt and pepper. After this has been cooking for a little, put in the smaller fish and cook until they dissolve. Strain the soup and add the big fish in the pot: cook for about a quarter of an hour. Finally, add the lemon juice.

Stelios Balamoutzos, Nea Alikarnassos

Boiled sardines

(Vrastes sardeles)

Boil some sardines and throw away the liquid. Serve them with lemon and oil.

M. Karefoulis, Heraklion

Octopus in wine

(Chtapodi krasato)

(for 5 persons)
1 kilo octopus
1 cup of oil
1 glass of red wine
1 lb. of tomatoes
2 or 3 laurel leaves
pepper

Wash and cut the octopus in small pieces. Put it in a pot with the oil and let it cook till the water has been absorbed.

Pour in the wine, let it bubble, add the

Fried whiting

crushed tomatoes, the laurel leaves, the pepper. Simmer.

Octopus with small pasta

(Chtapodi me makaroni kofto)

(for 6 persons)
1 kilo of octopus
1 lb. of small pasta
1 cup of oil, 1 onion
1 tbsp. of concentrated tomato pulp
1 tumbler of wine
salt and pepper

Wash and cut the octopus in pieces. Brown the onion in the oil and add the octopus. Let it cook absorbing its own water. Pour in the wine, and let it bubble. Then, add the tomato concentrate dissolved in a glass of water, salt and pepper.

When the octopus is cooked, remove it from the pot. Add some water to the pot and when it boils, add the small pasta. Serve the octopus with the pasta in the same dish.

Chariklia Charami, Plakalona, Kisamos.

Octopus with rice

(Chtapodi me ryzi)

See cuttlefish with rice.

Boiled Octopus

(Chtapodi vrasto)

1 kilo of octopus
1 cup of oil
2 or 3 cloves of garlic
1 small cup of vinegar
pepper, oregano

Wash the octopus and put it in a pot to boil without adding any water. Only add water if it has absorbed its own and isn't yet completely cooked. Then remove it from the fire, cut it up in small pieces. Beat the vinegar with the oil, the finely chopped garlic, the pepper and the oregano and pour this over the octopus.

Cuttlefish in wine

(Soupies me krasi)

(for 5 persons)
1 kilo of cuttlefish
1 cup of olive oil
2 or 3 onions
1 tbsp. concentrated tomato pulp
a tumbler of white wine
salt, pepper

Clean the cuttlefish: remove the eyes, the internal shell, or "bone", the stomach and the ink. Brown the chopped onion in oil, add the wine, the tomato concentrate dissolved in a glass of water, salt and pepper and let it boil. Add the chopped cuttlefish, stir, cook for a few minutes, add some water, enough to cover the fish, and simmer.

Eleni Kondoudaki, Kali Limenes.

Cuttlefish and spinach

(Soupies me spanaki)

(for 5 persons)
1 kilo of cuttlefish
1 kilo of spinach
1 cup of oil
2 onions

The fishing-boat comes into the port of Ierapetra. Crete 1940-1950, photo by Koutoulakis.

1 tumbler of white wine
a little dill
mint
salt
pepper

Clean the cuttlefish as above. Brown the onions in oil and add the dill, the mint and then add the chopped cuttlefish. When it is boiling, pour in the wine and let it bubble; add the salt and pepper, 2 glasses of water and simmer. Ten minutes before the food is cooked, add the spinach.

Eleni Kondoudaki, Kali Limenes.

Cuttlefish and rice

(Soupies me ryzi)

(for 6 persons)
1 kilo of cuttlefish
1 cup of oil
2 onions
1 tbsp. of concentrated tomato pulp
1 lb. of rice
salt
pepper

Clean, wash and chop the cuttlefish. Brown the chopped onions in the oil and add the cuttlefish. Let them cook a few minutes before adding the tomato concentrate dissolved in a glass of water, the pepper and salt; simmer for about an hour. Add water as needed to the pot and bring to the boil (you need to count 2 and a half cups of stock for one of rice): add the rice and stir at intervals until it is cooked.

Cuttlefish and potatoes

(Soupies me patates)

Just as in the former recipe, but instead of rice use potatoes.

Cuttlefish with rice-like pasta

(Soupies me kritharaki)

As above.

Chariklia Charami, Plakalona, Kisamos.

Balls made with octopus

(Chtapodokeftedes)

Wash and boil the octopus. Then place it in the deep freeze for a couple of hours. When it is frozen, mince it. Add bread crumbs, salt, pepper, parsley if desired, and shape the balls- although according to fishermen, the parsley may impair the taste of the octopus. Serve with a good strong white wine.

Antonis Englezakis, Heraklion.

Balls made with tuna

(Tonos Keftedes)

The same as above, having frozen the tuna fish so as to mince it.

Antonis Englezakis, Heraklion.

Crab

Fried squid

(Kalamarakia tiganita)

Clean and wash the squid, removing the eyes, the jelly from the back, the ink and the innards. Separate the tentacles from the stomach which is to be cut in round slices. Salt, pepper, flour and deep-fry in lots of oil.

Squid with tomatoes

(Kalamaria me tomata)

1 kilo of squid
1 cup of oil
1 or 2 onions
a small bunch of parsley
1 lb. of tomatoes
salt
pepper

Wash and clean the squid. Brown the onion in the oil and add the crushed tomatoes with the chopped parsley, salt and pepper. Let this cook for some time. Then add the squid, stir and simmer until the sauce thickens.

Chariclia Charami, Plakalona, Kisamos.

Moray with tomatoes

(Smirena me tomata)

As above.

Spiros Charamis, Heraklion.

WHITING

Long ago, salted whiting was one of the more common products of the fishing industry of Crete, and, naturally, it was to be found more often in the regions that were farthest from the sea. The price was accessible to everybody, hence its name of "ftochogiannis", which means: poor John, thereby implying that it is a food for the poor. It was prepared in many different ways, with all the other products of the Cretan land: with pulses, greens, cereals...

Whiting with flour and lemon

(Bakaliaros alevrolemono)

(for 5 persons)
800 grams of salted whiting
1 cup of oil
1 onion
1 lb. of potatoes
a little dill
a little parsley
pepper
2 or 3 tbsps of flour
the juice of 2 lemons

Desalt the whiting the night before, having cut it in slices and change the water a couple of times.

Brown the grated onion in some oil in a pot. Add 2 glasses of water, bring to the boil and add the dill, the parsley, the potatoes, cut in pieces: simmer. Then, carefully add the slices of whiting and the pepper and cook for another 20 minutes.

Dissolve the flour in a little warm water, add the lemon juice: mix this with the food. Bring to the boil and remove from the fire: the dish is ready.

Stefania Papadaki, Axos, Milopotamos.

Fried whiting

(Bakaliaros tiganitos)

(for 4 persons)
800 grams of whiting
1 cup of flour
1 glass of water
1 egg
a little salt

Desalt the whiting, leaving it in water from the day before. Make a batter with the water, the flour, the egg and a little salt.

Dip the whiting slices, one by one, in this batter and fry them in lots of hot oil.

Baked whiting

(Bakaliaros plaki)

(for 5 persons)
1 fillet of whiting
1 kilo of potatoes
2 finely chopped onions
2 or 3 cloves of garlic
1 lb. of tomatoes
1 cup of oil
a little oregano
a small bunch of parsley
salt, pepper

Desalt the whiting. Slice the potatoes and place them in a baking pan. Sprinkle them with salt, pepper, oregano and garlic. Then place the fish, sprinkling it in the same way;

Fishermen in the port of Heraklion. Removing the fish from the fishing-nets.

Lobster grilled.

finally, repeat the first step with the potatoes. Pour the crushed tomatoes and the oil over the whole dish and bake.

Maria Chalkiadaki, Heraklion

Whiting with potatoes

(Bakaliaros me patates)

(for 5 persons)
1 kilo whiting
1 cup of oil
2 onions
1 lb. of tomatoes
a small bunch of parsley
1 kilo of potatoes
salt
pepper

Brown the finely chopped onions in the oil adding the crushed tomatoes, the parsley, the salt and pepper. Let this cook, and later add the potatoes: when these are half cooked, add the desalted whiting and cook for another quarter of an hour or so.

M. Kiriakakis, Chania.

Crab pilaff

Crabs, lobster or scampi grilled

(Kavouria, astakos or karavides sti schara)

Boil the crabs, lobster or scampi in salted water. Then grill them gently on the charcoal.

Spiros Charamis, Heraklion.

Crab pilaff

(Kavropilafo)

Wash and boil the crabs. Strain them. Separate the feet and pound them. Place them in a colander, pour water over them and mix it with the water in which you boiled the crabs. Measure out the water to cook the rice (two and a half cups of liquid for one of rice).

SNAILS AND LENTEN FOOD

There are several fasting periods established by the Orthodox Church. During these fasts it is strictly forbidden to eat any meat and most products that derive from animals: therefore people eat a great variety of vegetables and wild greens. Modern dieticians maintain that all this has to do with the good health and physical well-being of the Cretans. The fasts are still kept nowadays and everybody can enjoy the wonderful tastes of the products in season: vetchling (papoules), milk worts (agalatsides), coast chicory (stamnagathi), chicories (radikia), centauries (askolybri) and the cultivated winter vegetables are among the many savoury greens which are consumed during Lent (right up to the Easter feast). Equally common are snails, pulses, olives and by the sea-side, though not on an every day basis, octopus, squid and cuttlefish: this last one, often cooked with greens, is a great Lent delicacy.

In the same manner, during the fasts that occur in summer, you get the vegetables of the season : tomato, naturally (tomato and rice, "tomatorizo" is the typical dish served in Cretan monasteries at this time of year), and again snails and different kinds of sea-food. The same happens during the fast before Christmas: frugal meals which keep all the flavour of the vegetables and the products of the season. On the other hand there are several more complex dishes which are prepared on the feast days that happen to fall during one or the other fasting periods: the feast of the Annunciation ("Evangelismos"), on the 25th of March, during Lent, the feast of the Transfiguration ("Metamorfosis"), on the 6th of August, during the fast before the Dormition of our Lady, and other feasts like the local ones of Patron Saints are among the most important ones. On these occasions the most common fare is fish, cooked in many different, original and delicious ways: on the coast, in the eastern part of the island, fish with ochra was usually prepared on the 6th of August, while in the village of Atsipopoulo in the province of Rethimnon, salted whiting with chickpeas was the usual fare on the day of the local patron saint, Ayios Eleftherios, a feast which occurs during the fast before Christmas, and therefore at a time of the year when housewives couldn't count on fresh fish, the weather being unpredictable. Another very common patron saint is Saint Nicholas and all the regions dedicated to him had the opportunity to enrich their fasting meals with other more special dishes: in the villages close to Sitia, for example, "kakavia" (fish soup) was always served on the 6th of December.

SNAILS

A common dish in Minoan Crete, especially in the country side: Minoan archaeological finds gave light to a vessel full of snails on the island of Santorini. It was a food easy to find, free of the toil and the uncertainty of hunting... In Ancient Greece it was the poor man's meal: snails were abundant and free of charge. Though those who were well-off also liked snails, "kochli" as they were known, or "chochli" as they are still called in Crete, where they've kept their ancient name. As Galinos (5, 669) tells us: "All Greeks eat them". During the Byzantine years, snails continued to be a favourite dish in all the Greek world, specially in Crete where, then as now, they were eaten with rice or ground wheat.

But snails weren't just a food to be eaten during the fasts: they constituted an excellent snack for wine or "tsikoudia" (raki). The "boubouristi" were by far the favourite ones: these are snails which are

Snails with "chondro"

deep fried in olive oil and then have vinegar poured over them (though there are a great many interesting techniques in the different ways of preparing "boubouristi")

To this day snails are cooked all through the year, after having been kept in clean sacks of a loose fabric, which lets the air in. But if they remain in the sacks too long, they become thinner and loose their taste.

It is said that the snails of Crete, especially those to be found on the mountains and in uncultivated areas, are the best. This is because the flora of the island is made of many aromatic herbs, which are the best food for snails and gives them this wonderful particular taste. According to the season, one can find a dozen different ways of cooking snails in Crete.

THE PREPARATION OF THE SNAILS

Snails are gathered and put away in loosely knit sacks, until they're to be cooked. One must remember that they're alive and therefore may die, for a number of reasons: a single dead one will ruin the enjoyment of a dish of snails because of the bad smell it exudes.

Snails must be carefully cleaned and the membrane covering the orifice must be removed: the larger the membrane, the larger and juicier the snail. Put them in water for a little while and you will immediately see them come back to life: one by one, they come out of their shells, making it easy to see if, by chance, there are any dead ones. With a pin try to get those that don't come out of their shells to react and, if they don't, discard them. In every case, let the snails boil in salted water until you can remove the froth (which is in fact their saliva). Then, clean them one by one, with a small knife, removing whatever bits of the membrane that may still be around the orifice or on the shell. Now the snails are ready to be cooked...

Snails with "chondros"

(for 6 persons)
1 kilo of snails
1 lb. of "chondros"(ground wheat)
2 cups of oil
2 onions
2 large zucchini

Cracking almonds open in Crete in 1950. Photograph by Kostas Koutoulakis.

4 ripe tomatoes
salt.

Boil and strain the snails. Change the water and boil for another 10 minutes. Rinse them in cold water, clean them and put them in the pot with the oil, the onions, the zucchini and the tomatoes, all chopped. Add 2 glasses of water and simmer for half an hour. Remove the snails from the pot and put them aside. Add plenty of water to the remaining sauce, and, when it boils, add the "chondros"(roughly ground wheat).Turn down the heat and stir constantly to keep the sauce from sticking. Once the "chondros" has cooked, return the snails to the pot, give a good stir and remove the pot from the fire.

Loula Metaxa, Heraklion.

Boiled snails

(Chochli vrasti)

1 kilo of snails
2 or 3 laurel leaves
5 or 6 pepper seeds (whole)
1 small tumbler of vinegar
salt
lemon.

Boiled snails are the most common dish during Lent, and especially during Holy Week, when oil is also forbidden. An excellent "meze" (snack) to accompany Cretan raki or "tsikoudia".

The snails are cleaned with the utmost care and put in pot, covered in water which is brought to the boil: the froth, which is nothing more than their saliva, can thus be removed. After having changed the water, add the salt, the vinegar, the laurel leaves, the pepper seeds and when this is boiling, add the snails. Let boil and cook and then serve.

Boiled snails

Boiled snails with oil and lemon or with oil and vinegar

(Chochli vrasti me ladolemono - ladoxido)

As above. Before serving, pour either oil and lemon or oil and vinegar over them.

Shepherd's snails

(Chochli voskitiki)

1 kilo snails
1 cup of oil
1 tbsp. of flour
the juice of 2 lemons

Clean, boil and strain the snails. Put them back in the pot with the oil, the lemon and the flour. Bring them to the boil and serve them.

Eleni Daouraki, Sitia.

Shepherd's snails

Snails "boubouristi"

1 kilo large snails
olive oil for frying
salt
vinegar

This is the most common way of preparing snails in Crete, especially when a group of friends gets together. It is an excellent "meze" for wine but also an equally appreciated snack for "tsikoudia".

The snails must be large (juicy) and after cleaning them, add them in the pot, head first. Fry them on a hot fire, stirring a couple of times. Then add some salt and some vinegar and they're ready.

Eleni Daouraki-Anipsitaki, Sitia.

Holy Thursday snails

(Chochli Megalis Pemptis)

(for 6-8 persons)
1 kilo of snails
1 kilo of zucchini
1 kilo artichoke hearts
1 kilo potatoes
oil for frying
2 or 3 lemons
salt
pepper.

On Holy Thursday, as opposed to the day before and the day after, olive oil is not forbidden. This dish was very common in the region of Mesara, where, even before the advent of green-houses, zucchini were to be had in the early spring.

Boil, strain and clean the snails. Cut the potatoes in large slices and fry them lightly in a pan: just enough to colour them , not to cook them. Slit open the zucchini and the artichokes and fry them, like the potatoes, in the pan. Add the snails to the pan for a few minutes. Now put all the ingredients in a large pot, including the frying oil, which is still hot and 2 cups of water. Salt, pepper, and, 2 minutes before the food is thoroughly cooked, remove from the fire and add the lemon juice.

Eleni Bitsakaki, Petrokefali, Heraklion.

Stew of snails

(Chochli stifado)

(for 4-5 persons)
1 kilo of snails
1 kilo of onions
a large cup of oil
1 lb. of ripe tomatoes, or
1 to 2 tbsps of concentrated tomato pulp diluted in water
5 or 6 laurel leaves
a small glass of wine
salt
pepper.

Boil and strain the snails. Brown the onions and add the chopped tomatoes, salt and pepper. Bring to the boil before adding the snails, the laurel leaves and the wine. Simmer until the sauce thickens.

Evang. Florou, Heraklion.

Snails "boubouristi"

Snails with artichokes and broad beans

Snails with artichokes and green broad beans

(Chochli me anginares ke koukia)

(for 6 persons)
1 kilo of snails
1 kilo of green broad beans
1 lb. of artichoke hearts
1 cup of oil
1 tbsp. of vinegar
1 tbsp. of flour
1 small bunch of fresh garlic leaves
salt , pepper

Boil and clean the snails. Brown them in the oil and then add the broad beans with a little water. Simmer until half cooked and then add the artichoke hearts, the salt and the pepper. Simmer and when almost done, take a little liquid from the pot to mix the flour and the vinegar before returning all this to the pot. Bring to the boil and serve.

Ch. Pattakou, Ayia Paraskevi, Amari.

Snails with rice

(Chochli me ryzi)

(for 6 persons)
1 kilo of snails
2 cups of rice
half a cup of olive oil
1 onion
3 large ripe tomatoes
salt, pepper.

Boil and strain the snails. Brown the finely chopped onion in a pot with the oil. Add the snails and, after a few minutes, the

Snails with rice

finely chopped tomatoes, salt and pepper. Bring to the boil, then remove the snails from the pot, add more water (about 5 cups), bring to the boil again and then add the rice. When the rice is half-cooked, return the snails to the pot. Simmer, stirring constantly and after a few minutes the food is ready.

Stefania Papadaki, Axos, Milopotamos.

«Simpetheria» with snails and aubergines

(for 6 persons)
1 kilo of snails
1 cup and a half of oil
1 onion
1 kilo of aubergines
1 cup of "xinochondro" (ground wheat and sour milk)
1 lb. of ripe tomatoes
salt and pepper

Cut the aubergines in small pieces, salt them and let them stand for one hour. Rinse them, strain them and fry them in the oil with the onion. Boil and clean the snails, then fry them a little before adding the pulped tomatoes: bring to the boil and simmer for a few minutes. Add 2 or 3 glasses of water to the pot and when boiling add the "xinochondro", some salt if needed and pepper. Simmer and stir regularly until cooked.

Kat. Papadaki, Chania.

Snails with zucchini and garlic

(Chochli me kolokithia ke skordo)

(for 5-6 persons)
1 kilo of large snails
1 kilo of zucchini

Snails with zucchini

1 lb. of potatoes
2 onions
a large cup of oil
1 kilo of tomatoes
5 or 6 cloves of garlic
salt, pepper.

A favourite summer dish all over the island.

Boil, strain and clean the snails.

Brown the onions in the oil and add the snails, the tomatoes, pepper and salt. Bring to the boil before adding the garlic, the potatoes and the zucchini, which have been slit open (that is, they're cut in four, but not all the way through, so as to remain in one piece). Simmer on a low fire.

Maria Fotinaki, Heraklion.

Snails with tomato

(Chochli me tomata)

The snails are cleaned, boiled and fried as above. Instead of vinegar, add chopped tomatoes and simmer till the sauce thickens. Add salt, pepper and serve. A few potatoes, too, can be added with the tomatoes.

Eleni Daouraki-Anipsitaki, Sitia.

"Simpetherio" with snails

GREENS - VEGETABLES

A great many edible plants form part of the Cretan flora, providing a cheap source of food. There always was a very strong tie between the Cretans of old and Nature, as can be seen on Minoan wall-paintings: a number of plants are represented, some played an important part in every day life, others in religion. Edible plants were a basic source of food in Minoan times, while other plants were objects of adoration: there are still dozens of trees in Crete which are known for their sacred character, a living proof, after all these centuries, of the close relationship Minoan Cretans had with Nature.

In the years that followed, greens and vegetables were the basic food of the poor and of those who cultivated the land. Some were eaten raw, just as they were picked from the fields, others boiled or cooked in different ways. We don't know how exactly Ancient Cretans cooked their greens.

The greens and vegetables Cretans used to eat were then, as they are today, of excellent quality. Raw greens were usually used in salads, as an accompaniment to the main dish. Here is a description of the greens used raw in salads:

Pumpkin pie

Coast chicory ("stamnagathi")

Vetchling ("papoules")

Coast chicory ("stamnagathi")

The Ancients, so Dioscouridis tells us, used it as a remedy. Today it is widely appreciated all over Crete and, once picked, is served with oil and vinegar. It is a thorny bush, but the thorns ("agathia" in Greek) aren't too prickly and the gathering of the small edible green leaves isn't so difficult. Its name goes back to an old custom in Crete where the water jars were covered with "stamnagathi" ("stamna" means crock) to prevent small animals from getting into the water. As with all salads in Crete, the preparation depends on the region and the imagination of the housewife: often, this green is mixed with other wild edibles, a little spring onion (using only the bulb) and dill.

Chicory, ("radikio")

A great delicacy: raw, it is always eaten with a shot of vinegar, because of its bitterness; boiled, with both oil and vinegar.

Milk wort ("agalatsida")

Known as "galaktitis" in Byzantium, as "galaktida" in the Middle Ages, it is a Cretan herb with a sweetish taste: delicious as a salad with Cretan olive oil, it can also be boiled or cooked with tomato.

Purslane ("glistrida")

In the rest of Greece this plant is more commonly known as "andrakla". A native plant of the island, it is also cultivated and is an appreciated summer ingredient to any salad: tomato, cucumber, or even egg and potato. Recent research has shown the plant's abilities to counteract cholesterol, thanks to its proteins: it is therefore an excellent and wholesome edible.

Vetchling ("papoules")

This plant is also known as "psares" or "kambilies", in Crete. It is a cultivated green, used almost always raw, in salads.

Cauliflower in egg-and-lemon sauce

salad with purslane

Spinach pies

Its taste is slightly bitter, and it is most common during Lent. It is eaten with oil and vinegar, though on the fasting days when oil is forbidden, it is eaten with plain salt. Like raw artichokes, it is also a very common snack ("mezes") taken with "tsikoudia" (or "raki").

GREENS IN PASTRY ("Chortopites")

Crete was, and continues to be, famous for its use of greens in pastry. It used to be a winter and springtime preparation, due to the abundance of fresh greens in the countryside. During summer it was next to impossible to find wild greens to make the pies; so Cretan housewives prepared them with cultivated greens. In the village of Atsipopoulo, in the region of Rethimnon, "chortopites" were made with the tender shoots of wild beets ("vlita"), which grow profusely in all Cretan gardens.

There are a great number of different kinds of pies made with greens: in each part of the island they are prepared with all sorts of different ingredients and in all kinds of shapes. According to the local custom, these pies can be large, medium or small. Cretan pies have always had a unique taste, because their stuffing is made of a rich mixture of wild greens and aromatic herbs. To achieve the right balance between these two was a delicate operation: Cretan housewives, using their experience and their own taste, were able to produce pies with a light smell and a clean taste, where each herb or green was distinct. In some regions, strong aromatic herbs were not used at all.

Grilled ("ofti") salad

Take as many potatoes, onions and olives (preferably of the kind known as "stafidoelies") as you want. Roll them all up in grease proof or aluminium paper and place on the embers to cook. When ready, peel the potatoes and the onions, cut them in slices, and, with the olives, serve them in a

Centauries

dish with lemon and oil and salt. This is a meal by itself, but may also be served as an accompaniment to other traditional dishes.

Amalia Kornarou, Rethimnon.

Potato and egg salad

(Salata me patates ke avga)

(for 4-5 persons)
1 kilo of potatoes
5 or 6 eggs
2 tomatoes, 1 onion
2 tbsp. of finely chopped parsley
1 cucumber
a handful of olives
1 cup of oil
2 tbsps of vinegar
salt
pepper

Wash and boil the potatoes, then peel them. Boil the eggs and cut them and the potatoes in slices, add the sliced tomatoes, the finely chopped onion, the parsley, the sliced cucumber and the olives. Mix with salt, pepper, oil and vinegar.

Salad with beetroots

(Pantzaria salata)

(for 5-6 persons)
1 kilo beetroots
4 or 5 crushed cloves of garlic
half 1 lb. of strained yoghurt
1 cup of roughly ground walnuts
1 cup of oil, salt
a tiny glass of vinegar (2 tbsps)

- Rice and cabbage

- Cabbage "dolmades"

Boil the beets, clean them and dice them. Beat the oil with the vinegar and the yoghurt, the garlic and the walnuts and pour this over the beets. Add some salt, mix and let the salad stand in the refrigerator for an hour or so before serving.

Purslane salad

(Glistrida salata)

1 lb. of purslane
half a lb. of strained yoghurt
a little oil
2 or 3 crushed cloves of garlic
the juice of one lemon
salt

Clean, wash and chop the purslane. Beat the oil with the lemon, the garlic, the yoghurt, and pour over the salad. Add some salt and chill it in the refrigerator.

Boiled bulbs of grape hyacinth

(Askordoulaki vrasti)

1 kilo of "askordoulaki"
a small bunch of dill
2 or 3 garlic leaves
salt, oil, vinegar

Peel the bulbs, like onions, and wash them in a bowl with water. Boil them twice, changing the water. The third time, add salt to the water and when they are cooked, strain them. Finely chop the garlic leaves and the dill, add to the bulbs; then pour the oil and vinegar mixture and stir.

Stelios Balamoutzos, Heraklion.

Rice and cabbage

(Lachanoryzo)

(for 5-6 persons)
1 cabbage
1 lb. of rice
1 cup of oil
1 lb. of tomatoes
1 onion, salt, pepper.

Cut the cabbage in small pieces. Brown the finely chopped onion in the oil. Add the crushed tomato, bring to the boil, add the cabbage and the rice, and 3 cups of water. Salt and pepper. Simmer, adding water if needed.

Stefania Papadaki, Axos, Milopotamos.

Stuffed cabbage leaves

(Lachanodolmades)

(for 5-6 persons)
1 cabbage
a small bunch of parsley
mint
fennel leaves
1 lb. of rice
4 tomatoes
2 cups of oil

3 onions
salt, pepper

Cut off the stalk, separate the leaves of the cabbage and bleach them. Prepare the stuffing with all the ingredients mentioned above. Take each leave, separate it in 2 parts, removing the central vein, place one spoonful on the edge of each half and roll in round or triangular shapes. Place the "dolmades" in circles in a pot, Add water, 2 tbsps of oil and simmer. Now and then, shake the pot to keep the lower cabbage leaves from sticking.

(If desired, some of the rice can be left out and some minced meat added.)

Argiro Manousaki, Boulgaro, Kisamos.

Stuffed zucchini flowers

(Anthi kolokithias gemisti)

(for 5-6 persons)
Zucchini flowers
1 lb. of rice
1 cup of oil
1 lb. ripe tomatoes
1 onion, salt, pepper, parsley, mint and fennel

The flowers have to be picked in the morning so that they will be open. Wash them and prepare the stuffing: Chop the

Page 108 "Yemista": tomatoes, aubergines, zucchini.
Page 109 -Stuffed zucchini flowers -«Dolmades» in vine leaves

parsley, the mint, the fennel leaves, the onions and the tomatoes, very finely. Add the oil, the rice, the salt and pepper and water: mix. Instead of all the rice, you can use half the quantity and add half 1 lb. of minced meat.

Stuff the flowers and place them in a pot. Cover them in water, put a plate over them to keep them from opening and let them simmer.

Rita Koutantou, Axos, Milopotamos.

Stuffed vine leaves

(dolmades me ampelofila)

(for 5-6 persons)
1 lb. of vine leaves
1 lb. of rice
2 or 3 artichoke hearts
2 onions
2 or 3 zucchini
2 potatoes
2 cups of oil
1 lemon
salt
pepper
mint.

Bleach the vine leaves. Strain them and prepare the stuffing.

Place the rice in a bowl. Grate the potatoes, the zucchini, the onions, the artichoke hearts: add all this to the rice. Mix with the finely chopped mint, the salt and pepper and the oil.

Stuff the vine leaves and place them in a pot. Put a plate over them, cover with water and simmer gently. Just before removing them from the fire, pour the lemon juice over them.

Maria Xilouri, Heraklion.

Vine leaves and artichokes

(Dolmades me anginares)

The same as above, but you alternate layers of "dolmades" with layers of artichokes, cleaned and whole.

Voula Daskalaki, Chania.

Stuffed vegetables

(Yemista)

(for 5-6 persons)
5 or 6 tomatoes
2 or 3 aubergines
2 or 3 zucchini
2 or 3 green peppers
2 or 3 potatoes, 2 onions
dill, parsley
1 cup of "staka" (fresh goat's butter)
1 cup of oil
salt
pepper
1 lb. of rice
1 tbsp. of concentrated tomato pulp diluted in 1 glass of water
1 cup grated cheese

Hollow out all the vegetables and chop their contents (except for the green peppers) in a bowl. Add the finely chopped onion, the "staka" butter, the dill, the parsley, the rice, salt and pepper. Salt the empty insides of the vegetables, stuff them and place them in a baking pan. Pour the tomato concentrate and a cup of oil over them. Cook in a hot oven. Just before turning off the oven, sprinkle with the grated cheese and let this melt.

Katina Koutsaki, Kali Limenes.

Artichokes - Nuns

(Anginares kalogres)

(for 4 persons)
10 to 12 artichokes
salt

- Artichokes (kalogres)

-Stalks of wild greens in flour and lemon

- Zucchini "sfuggato"
-Artichokes "sfuggato"

pepper
1 cup of oil
1 little onion
1 glass of water
1 glass of milk or 4 tbsps of cream

Clean the artichokes and cut an incision in the shape of a cross on the upper side of each. Sprinkle a little salt and pepper in the inside of each artichoke. Brown the finely chopped onion in the oil, add the water and then the artichokes upside down. (If you like you can sprinkle them with bread crumbs). When they are nearly cooked, pour the milk or the cream over them. Don't stir the artichokes, just shake the pot now and then during the cooking.

Ergin. Atsalaki, Rousapidia, Merambello.

Zucchini with eggs

(Kolokithia me avga)

(for 4-5 persons)
1 lb. of zucchini
1 lb. of tomatoes
1 cup of oil
1 onion
salt
pepper
5 eggs

Cut the zucchini in round slices and brown them with the finely chopped onion in a pan with oil. Add the tomatoes, the salt and pepper: simmer. When the zucchini are cooked, beat the eggs and add them to the pan. Stir and let the eggs cook.

Evangelia Katsanevaki, Askyfou, Sfakia.

Artichokes with yoghurt

(Anginares me yiaourti)

(for 4 persons)
1 kilo of artichoke hearts
1 onion
1 cup of oil
salt
pepper
1 lb. of yoghurt

Brown the onion in the oil, add the artichoke hearts, a little water, pepper and salt and cook till the artichokes are tender. Then, add the yoghurt, stir and remove from the fire.

Artichokes «sfuggato»

Boil 1 kilo of artichokes in salted water and strain them. Brown the artichokes in hot oil until their water is evaporated. Beat 5 or 6 eggs, add salt and pepper and pour them over the artichokes. When the eggs are firm, turn the "sfuggato" around with the help of a large plate and cook on the other side.

Eleni Anipsitaki-Daouraki, Sitia.

-Zucchini pie
- Zucchini "balls"

Zucchini pie from Chania

(Kolokithoboureko chaniotiko)

(for 7-8 persons)
2 kilos of zucchini cut in fine round slices
3 potatoes cut in fine round slices
salt, pepper, mint
1 kilo of "mizithra" (cottage cheese)
1 cup of olive oil
For the **dough**:

1 small cup of olive oil, the juice of 1 lemon, 1 glass of water, a little salt, 1 lb. of flour.

Oil a baking pan and place all the salted ingredients in layers. That is first potatoes, then "mizithra" and mint, the third layer with zucchini, the fourth "mizithra" and mint, the fifth potatoes, the sixth "mizithra" and mint and so on. When all the ingredients have been used, place a simple layer of dough over the baking pan, sprinkle with oil (1 cup) and sesame seeds. Before baking it, mark the portions with a knife.

Katina Lytinaki, Myloniana, Kydonia.

Zucchini pie

(Kolokithopita)

(for 7-8 persons)
2 kilos of zucchini
3 glasses of milk
1 cup of oil
750 grams of feta cheese
3 eggs
3 cups of semolina, salt

Cut the zucchini in fine round slices, salt them and let them stand. Once they've got rid of most of their liquid, strain them, mix them with the other ingredients, place them in a buttered pan and bake the pie.

Maria Bitsakaki, Heraklion.

Large spinach-and-greens pie

(Chortopita)

(for 6 persons)
1 kilo of spinach and other greens
1 cup of oil
salt, pepper, mint, sesame seeds
2 onions
half a kilo of flour
1 glass of water
1 small cup of oil, salt

Use the following greens: wild carrots (stafilinaki), bur chervils (kafkalides), corn poppies (koutsounades), milkworts (galatsides), saw thistles (tsochi), wild fennel (maratha), baby leeks (prasakia) and spinach. Chop them all roughly and brown them in oil with the onion: add salt, pepper and mint.

Warm the water and add the small cup of oil, a little salt and the flour as needed to make a dough. Roll it out and spread a very thin layer of this dough in the bottom of the baking pan: on this, spread a thin layer of the fried greens. Repeat the operation: a layer of paper-thin dough, a layer of thinly spread greens, until all the ingredients are used. Finish with a layer of dough, dab with egg, sprinkle with sesame seeds and bake.

(Cheese-feta- may be added to the mixture of greens and spinach)

Maria Koulizaki, Platanias, Chania.

Small spinach-and-greens pasties

(Chortopitakia)

Brown all the greens as in the above recipe and strain them. Prepare the same dough and roll it open: with a saucer, cut out circular pieces and on each piece place 1 tbsp. of mixture, fold it and close the edges firmly, pressing them down with a fork. Deep-fry the pasties.

Spinach pie

Spinach pie

(Spanakopita)

(for 6 persons)

Stuffing:
1 kilo and a half of spinach
1 cup of oil
1 onion
1 lb. of feta cheese
4 eggs
salt, pepper.

Dough:
half a cup of oil
the juice of one lemon
a little yeast (30 grams)
salt
1 glass of water
1 lb. of flour

Dilute the yeast in warm water, add the oil, the salt, the lemon juice and the flour: knead the dough and let it stand for a couple of hours.

In the meantime, prepare the stuffing. Chop the spinach and the onion very fine and brown them in the oil. When it is cooked, strain it and add the feta, some salt, pepper and the beaten eggs.

Roll out the dough and spread half of it in the bottom of a buttered baking pan, place the stuffing on top and, over the stuffing, the other half of the dough. Brush the top with butter and bake in the oven until golden and crisp.

Sofia Kaliontzi, Ierapetra.

Spinach pie

(Spanakoboureko)

(for 6-8 persons)
A good kilo of chopped spinach
half a kilo of sour "mizithra" (cottage cheese)
3 eggs
salt
pepper
nutmeg
half a kilo of paper-thin pastry

Chop the spinach, salt it and let it stand overnight. Next morning, drain it and brown it in butter until the water evaporates. Add the mashed "mizithra" and the eggs, a little grated nutmeg and some pepper. Butter 4 or 5 sheets of pastry, place some of the stuffing on the edge and roll up the pastry lenghtwise. In the same manner, roll up the rest of the pastry with the stuffing and place each roll, one next to the other, in the baking pan. Brush with fresh butter and bake till golden.

Maria Xiroudaki-Thalassinou,
Heraklion.

Fried pumpkin

(Glikokolokitha tiganiti)

Slice the pumpkin in long narrow pieces 2 to 3 cms thick. Salt them and put them in a sieve. Then dip each piece in flour and fry on a hot fire. Add either lemon juice or vinegar: that is, once all the slices have been fried, add a small cup of vinegar-or lemon juice- to the hot oil in the pan and then pour the mixture over the pumpkin pieces.

Chris. Pattakou, Ayia Paraskevi,
Amari.

Pumpkin patties

(Kolokithopitakia)

Stuffing:
2 or 3 kilos of pumpkin
3 or 4 eggs (optional)
2 onions
2 cups of grated cheese (optional)
salt, pepper, cumin

The dough:
1 kilo of flour
2 glasses of water
2 teasps salt
2 teasps oil
1 teasp. vinegar

Cut the pumpkin in slices and brown it with the finely chopped onion in the oil. Stir the pumpkin until it melts and until all the water has evaporated. Drain it and add the other ingredients.

Knead the dough, roll it out and prepare the pasties as usual (see Spinach-and-greens pasties).

Maria Bitsakaki, Heraklion.

Zucchini pie

(Kolokithopita me prasina kolokithia)

(for 6 persons)
1 kilo of zucchini
2 cups of milk
1 cup of butter or olive oil
3 eggs
1 cup grated cheese, salt

Grate the zucchini and salt them.

Beat the butter with the eggs, the milk

Pumpkin patties

and the cheese until you get a thick mash. Butter a baking pan, spread the grated zucchini and the mash on top: bake in a moderate oven for about an hour.

Efi Varveraki, Heraklion.

Pumpkin pie

(Glikokolokithopita)

(for 8 persons)
1 kilo and a half of pumpkin
2 onions
salt, pepper, mint
1 lb. of feta cheese
2 or 3 eggs

The dough:
1 cup of butter
1 cup of oil
2 eggs
salt
1 cup of milk
1 teasp. of baking powder
as much flour as needed

Brown the pumpkin and the onion and cook till mushy. Drain and add mint, grated feta and the eggs. Prepare the dough and roll it open. Spread half of it in a buttered baking pan, spread the mixture, and on the top the second half of the dough. Bake till golden.

Eleni Simitzi, Rethimnon.

Onion pasties

(Kromidokalitsouna)

1 kilo of onions cut in fine slices
3 roughly chopped tomatoes
100 grams feta cheese
1 cup of olive oil
salt
pepper

For the dough:
1 lb of flour
1 glass of water
1 small glass of olive oil
salt, tje juice of 1 lemon.

Brown the onions in the oil and add the tomatoes, salt and pepper, and, if you like, the crumbled feta. When cooked take it off the fire.

Knead the dough, roll it out and cut out round portions with a saucer. Put 1 tbsp. of the mixture in each round portion and close the pastry, forming semi-circular small pies. Deep-fry.

Maria Koulizaki, Platanias, Chania.

Artichokes and broad beans

(Anginares me koukia)

(for 6 persons)
1 kilo of artichokes
1 kilo of fresh broad beans
1 cup of oil
2 fresh garlic heads
1 small bunch of dill or fennel
salt
2 tbsps of flour
2 or 3 tbsps of vinegar

Clean the artichokes and the beans. Put the oil in a pot and then add the beans and 2 glasses of water. Let this boil for a quarter of an hour and then add the artichokes, the finely chopped garlic, the finely chopped fennel or dill and the salt. When the food is almost cooked, take some of the liquid which you gently add to the flour diluted in some water. Add the vinegar and pour this thick batter back into the pot, shaking the pot to mix the batter properly with the food. Simmer for a little before drawing the pot away from the fire.

Loula Metaxa, Heraklion.

Artichokes with broad beans

Leeks in lemon and flour sauce

(Prasa alevrolemono)

(for 4-5 persons)

Leeks, in Greek "prasa", are also called "kendanes" in Crete.

Clean 1 kilo of leeks, chop them and brown them in a cup of oil. Add a small bunch of finely chopped fennel leaves and a little salt: let this simmer. Dilute half a tbsp. of flour in a small cup of lemon juice, add to the pot, stir and cook for a few more minutes.

M. Kiriakakis, Chania.

Leeks with tomato

(Prasa me tomata)

(for 4-5 persons)

Clean, chop and brown 1 kilo of leeks as above. Add a small bunch of finely chopped celery and salt, then add 1 lb. of skinned and chopped ripe tomatoes: let this simmer until cooked.

Both in this recipe and in the preceding one (leeks with lemon and flour), you can add potatoes and snails.

Voula Daskalali, Chania.

Cauliflower in an egg and lemon sauce

(Kounoupidi avgolemono)

(for 4-5 persons)

Separate the flowers, wash them and brown them in oil. Add enough water to cover, salt and pepper and cook the cauliflower. Remove from the fire. Beat 2 eggs with the juice of 2 lemons and add a little of the liquid: return to the pot and mix.

Chrisoula Pattakou, Ayia Paraskevi, Amari.

Omelette with cauliflower

(kounoupidi sfougato)

Boil the cauliflower in salted water and strain it. Brown it in a pan with oil, turning it round until all the water evaporates.

Beat 4 or 5 eggs with some salt and pepper, and pour over the cauliflower. When the eggs are firm, turn the "sfuggato" upside down with the help of a large plate and cook on the other side.

Eleni Anipsitaki-Daouraki, Sitia.

Fried cauliflower

(Kounoupidi tiganito)

Cut the cauliflower and boil in salted water till it is slightly underdone. Strain it and separate the flowers. Prepare a thick batter with 3 eggs, 1 cup of grated cheese, salt, 1 tbsp. of oil and some flour. Heat oil in a pan, dip each flower in the batter and deep-fry.

Kat. Theodoraki, Rethimnon.

Fresh beans

(Fasolakia freska)

(for 4-5 persons)

1 kilo fresh beans

1 cup of oil, 1 onion

1 lb. of ripe tomatoes

salt, pepper
1 tbsp. of "staka" butter

Clean and wash the beans. Brown them in a pan with the oil and the onion. Add the crushed tomatoes, salt, pepper: simmer. Just before removing from the fire, add the "staka".

Manolis Stratakis, Heraklion.

Mushrooms and potatoes

(Manitaria me patates)

(for 4-5 persons)
1 kilo of mushrooms
1 cup of olive oil
1 lb. of ripe tomatoes
1 lb. of potatoes
salt, pepper, cinnamon
2 or 3 laurel leaves

Brown the mushrooms in the oil and then add the skinned and crushed tomatoes. Bring to the boil. Add the potatoes, salt and pepper, cinnamon and the laurel leaves. Cook.

Chris. Pattakou, Ayia Paraskevi, Amari.

"Sofagada" or "sofegada"

This is a wholesome Cretan dish which seems to have its origin in Venetian times. The word "sofegada" occurs in some texts of the time and experts believe it was originally some kind of meat dish. What we do know is that it was evidently cooked in its own steam, "suffocated", if we are to believe its Venetian etymology. The word has survived in Eastern Crete, though not to describe a meat dish. On the contrary, this is a dish based on garden produce, as we shall see further on. In Western Crete the name is unknown: some elderly people vaguely remember it, but have forgotten its meaning.

Until recently, it was prepared with the last produce of the garden at the end of summer. In the autumn, there were less quantities of vegetables and the gardener who found his daily nourishment in the produce of his garden, had to make do with whatever there was: 2 zucchini, 1 aubergine...Having no choice but to cook this, and on discovering that the result was satisfactory, "sofegada" became a very pleasant summer dish, also prepared when there is an abundance of vegetables.

«Sofegada»

Ingredients:

Aubergines, zucchini, fresh beans, green peppers (about 250 grams of each kind, leaving out any vegetable we don't

Pulses in the market in Heraklion

like), a few green beet leaves, zucchini flowers, potatoes, 1 kilo of tomatoes, 2 onions, 2 cups of oil, salt, pepper.

Brown the sliced onion in the oil. Add the zucchini, the beans, the aubergines cut in chunks. After a while, add the green peppers, the finely chopped tomatoes, the sliced potatoes and finally the flowers with the chopped green beet leaves. Salt, pepper, a little water and simmer for about one hour.

Loula Metaxa, Heraklion.

Zucchini balls

(Kolokithokeftedes)

(for 6 persons)
1 kilo of zucchini
1 lb. of potatoes
1 kilo of onions
2 or 3 eggs
1 cup of grated cheese
a little salt

Boil, and then strain, the zucchini, the potatoes and the onions. Work them into the eggs, the cheese, add the salt and shape the balls. Dip them in flour and deep-fry.

Voula Daskalaki, Chania.

Zucchini with garlic

(Kolokithia me skordo)

(for 6 persons)
1 kilo and a half of small zucchini
7 or 8 cloves of garlic, finely chopped
parsley
1 cup of oil
salt
pepper

Wash the zucchini and slit them with a knife. Put garlic in the slit and place the zucchini in a baking pan. Add the oil and the grated tomato, sprinkle with parsley, the salt and pepper and bake for an hour in a moderate oven.

Amalia Kornarou, Rethimnon.

Aubergines with rice

(Melitzanes me ryzi)

(for 6 persons)
1 lb. of aubergines

."Loubounia"

1 cup of oil
1 onion
3 tomatoes
1 cup of rice
4 glasses of water
salt, pepper

Brown the onion in the oil and add the sliced aubergines. Add the crushed tomatoes, let this come to the boil and then pour the water, salt and pepper. When the water boils, add the rice and finish cooking.

Niki Giannikaki, Therisos, Kydonia.

PULSES

Pulses have been known and have been included in the every day diet since Antiquity. Minoans used to make offerings of pulses and cereals to their gods, to show their gratitude for the fertility of the earth: the seeds planted and nourished by the earth were returned manifold. Some telling customs have remained with us to this day: the habit Cretan peasants have of cooking together all the kinds of pulses once a year goes way back to the most remote Antiquity. Every member of the family partakes of this mixture of pulses, then the animals of the house and finally a handful is flung onto the roof of the house, for the birds.

Civilisation took a great step forward with the systematic cultivation of cereals and pulses: these could be stored, providing nourishment on the days when, for one reason or another (weather, illness), it proved impossible to go out in search of food.

In more recent years, the ways of preparing pulses were very varied: each dish related to the local produce and so very often pulses were cooked with meat. These local customs, among other things, have a definite folkloric value.

Lupins

(Loubounia)

These beans were famous in Antiquity and were called "thermos". They have been in use in the Greek world since the most remote Antiquity; they were the usual fare of the cynical philosophers in Ancient Greece, they also were the main dish of the "dinners of Hecate": on the last day of every month, once the houses had been thoroughly cleaned, the table was set and Hecate's dinner served so as to placate the goddess of ghosts. In front of each house the dinner was placed on a tripod (the goddess was always figured on a tripod): any passer-by was welcome to this dinner, so naturally all the poor people waited impatiently for this occasion. Ever since, these beans have been identified as the poor man's fare.

Ancient Greeks prepared lupins, or "thermos", in exactly the same way as they do in Crete nowadays: first, they are boiled, then they're left in sea-water for 2 or 3 days to get rid of their bitterness.

They're served during the fasts, with olives and rusks.

Soaked broad beans

(Vrechtokoukia)

An indispensable dish during the fasts imposed by the Orthodox Church, especially on the days when it is forbidden to consume oil. Until recently, these beans were always served on "Kathari Deftera" (the Monday after Carnival, the first day of Lent). They too are one of the most common snacks ("mezes") that accompany a glass of "tsikoudia" (Crete's traditional form of spirits.)

No particular preparation is required: just soak the beans overnight, in salted water, in an earthenware or metal container. Next morning they're ready to be eaten, usually with some olives (of the kind called in Crete "alatsolies" or "stafidoelies") and some rusks ("paximadi").

«Palikaria»

(a mixture of many pulses)

They're also known as "psarokolyva" and "mayeria". This mixture of pulses is a very old custom, reminiscent of the "panspermia" known in Ancient Greece, reminiscent, too, of the Minoan offerings to the gods. For all we know it might go back to pre-historical times, for which there are no written sources. In Ancient Greece "panspermia" was an offering to the gods: to Apollo on the 7th day of the "Pyanepsonios", to "Chthonios" Hermes (Mercury of the Underworld) and to the dead during the "Anthestiria"; it was also prepared on the day of "Chytri" and during the feast of "Thargilia". A few of all the new seeds were boiled together and offered to the gods in gratitude for the plentiful new crops. This dish was served at the table of every Ancient Greek family and every member partook of it.

In Crete, this custom survived through the centuries. In the eastern part of the island, this dish was known as "palikaria", a word which may well derive from the ancient name: "polisporia" (which means: many seeds). It was cooked on the 5th of January, the day before the feast of the Baptism of Christ. All the family and the animals of the house shared this meal, in particular the animals used for farming. On this day, the old women in the region of Pediada still fling a plateful of this mixture on to the roof of the houses, for the birds. On this occasion men and animals share the same meal....

In some Cretan villages, "palikaria" or "polisporia" are prepared on the eve of the feast of the Epiphany (the Baptism of Christ and the Blessing of the Waters) and during Lent. The only difference is that the pulses are served with oil, finely

"Palikaria"

chopped parsley and fresh onion.

To prepare this dish: take a handful of all the kinds of pulses, broad beans, chick peas, beans, lentils, millet and a handful of wheat. Put them all in water overnight, except for the beans which have to be cleaned peeling the part where the bean sprouts and the lentils which need much less time to cook. Next day boil all the pulses together, except for the lentils again which are added 1/2 hour before the rest are ready. Then strain them and serve them in soup plates, with oil, a sprinkling of finely chopped dill and fresh onion. A wholesome and savoury dish, which takes us back to the most remote Greek antiquity...

Boiled broad beans

(Koukia vrasta)

(for 5 persons)
1 lb. of broad beans
olive oil
salt, lemon

Remove the black tips of the beans. Place them overnight in salted water. Next day, boil them in plain water for half an hour. Change the water and continue boiling them in fresh water, with the lid on, on a low flame. Towards the end the water is almost gone, so you need to stir the beans often. Bleach them with a little lemon juice and when they have absorbed all the water, remove the pot from the fire. Serve with oil and, if desired, with finely chopped dill and fresh onion.

Eleni Anipsitaki-Daouraki, Sitia.

Dried beans stewed with tomato

(Fasolia xera yachnista)

(for 6 persons)
1 lb. of beans
1 onion
1 cup of oil
1 or 2 tbsps of concentrated tomato pulp
2 or 3 sprigs of celery
half a small bunch of parsley
2 or 3 medium-sized carrots
salt
pepper

Soak the beans in water overnight. Next day, boil them in a pot until half cooked: then strain them. In another pot brown the onion with the oil and add the celery and the parsley finely chopped, the carrots cut in round slices or diced, the tomato concentrate diluted in water, salt and pepper. When all this comes to the boil, add the beans and simmer.

Dried beans in flour and lemon

(Fasolia xera alevrolemono)

(for 6 persons)
1 lb. of beans
1 cup of oil
1 tbsp. of flour
1-2 onions
1 lemon
salt
pepper

Soak the beans as above. Next day, boil them with the onions. Half way through, add the oil and the salt. In the meantime, dissolve the flour in the lemon juice and add it to the pot a little before the beans have cooked. The consistency should be that of a soup.

"Boiled broad beans"

Dried beans and rice

(Fasouloryzo)

This was not, generally speaking, a main course dish in Crete. It was simply a way of using up the left-over beans. For the sake of variety, rice was added, giving the dish another taste.

After having half cooked 1 cup of rice in water, the beans were added and the rice cooked through.

Since this is a savoury and wholesome dish, we don't need to have left-over beans to prepare it. First cook the beans. Remove them from the pot and in their own liquid cook the rice, adding a little water. Finally, add the beans with the rice and stir.

Broad beans

Broad beans stewed with tomato

(Koukia yachnista)

(for 6 persons)
1 lb. of beans
2 onions
2 tomatoes
1 cup of olive oil
a small bunch of parsley
1 teasp. of cumin
3 or 4 laurel leaves, salt
pepper

Soak the beans in water overnight. Remove the black tips, boil them for half an hour and drain them. Brown the finely chopped onions in the oil and add the tomatoes, also chopped, the parsley, the cumin, the laurel leaves, the salt and the pepper. Then add the boiled beans. Simmer till the sauce thickens.

Eleni Anipsitaki-Daouraki, Sitia.

Broad beans with potatoes

(Koukia me patates)

Just as above, adding a few potatoes, diced, when the tomatoes are simmering.

Eleni Anipsitaki-Daouraki, Sitia.

Dried broad beans with wild artichokes

(Koukia me agrianginares)

(for 6 persons)
1 lb. of dried broad beans
1 kilo of wild artichokes
1 small bunch of fennel
1 onion, 3 or 4 tomatoes
1 cup of oil
salt, pepper.

Broad beans and artichokes

Simmer the broad beans for half an hour and then strain them.

Brown the onion in the oil, add the tomato, the salt and pepper, the wild artichokes and the fennel. When this comes to the boil, add the boiled broad beans and cook until ready.

Kat. Koutsaki, Kali Limenes.

Yellow lentil puree

(Fava)

(for 4 persons)
2 cups of yellow lentils (split peas)
4 glasses of water, oil, salt.

Boil in salted water, very slowly till mushy. The lid must not sit tightly because the yellow lentil expands and can spill. Serve the puree with oil, raw onion and olives.

"Married" yellow lentil puree

(Fava ... pandremeni)

the left-over puree
1 onion
1 cup olive oil
4 tomatoes
cumin, salt, pepper

When there was some "fava" left, it was neither discarded nor was it served again: a completely new dish was prepared on its basis. This is one example of the creativity typical of the Cretan housewives, always finding new means for producing new dishes with new tastes. The expression "to marry the 'fava'" was common in the region of Sitia.

Finely chop the onion, brown it in the oil, add the skinned and chopped tomatoes, the cumin, the pepper. Simmer until all this melts, then add the "fava". Cook a little

longer, serve.

Eleni Anipsitaki-Daouraki, Sitia.

Chick peas stewed with tomato

(Revithia yachnista)

(for 6 persons)
1 lb. of chick peas
1 cup of oil
1 onion
1 lb. of ripe tomatoes or tomato concentrate
salt, pepper

Soak the peas overnight and on the following day brown them in the oil with the onion. Add the tomato, salt, pepper and water. Simmer.

-Chick peas with flour and lemon
-Dried beans
-Lentil soup

Chick peas with lemon and flour

(Revithia alevrolemono)

(for 6 persons)
1 lb. of chick peas
1 cup of oil
2 lemons
1 tbsp. of flour
salt, pepper

Soak the chick peas overnight in salted water. Next day, rinse them carefully and add them to the pot where you have browned the onion. Then, add water, salt, pepper and simmer. Mix the lemon juice with the flour and ten minutes before the peas are cooked, add the mixture to the pot.

Lentil soup

(Fakes soupa)

(for 6 persons)
1 lb. of lentils
1 cup of oil
1 tbsp. of tomato concentrate
1 onion
2 or 3 cloves of garlic
3 laurel leaves
half a small tumbler of vinegar
salt
pepper

Fill a pot with plenty of water. Add the lentils and bring to the boil. Drain the lentils. Brown the finely chopped onion in the oil, add the lentils, the garlic, the tomato concentrate dissolved in water, salt, pepper, the laurel leaves and more water if needed. Cook the lentils and a little before they are ready, put in the vinegar...

«Keftedes» made of «fava»

(yellow lentil balls)

1 lb. of "fava"
1 onion
a small bunch of parsley
1 cup of bread-(or rusk) crumbs
a handful of grated cheese
2 eggs
flour
oil for frying
salt
pepper

Boil the "fava" as usual. Let it cool, then add the grated onion, the finely chopped parsley, the crumbs, the cheese, 2 beaten eggs, salt, pepper. Mix with the yellow lentil and shape the balls, more long than round. Dip them in flour and deep-fry them.

Titika Miraki, Ayios Myronas, Malevizi

Chick peas balls

(Rovithokeftedes)

Basically the same as above: the chick peas, once they are cooked, are put through the mill. Then proceed as above.

Beans with fennel

(Fasolia me maratho)

(for 6 persons)
half a kilo of dried beans
1 cup of olive oil
300 grams of fennel
1 onion
1 spoonful of concentrated tomato pulp
salt
pepper.

Soak the beans in salted water overnight. Next day boil them for half an hour and then drain them. Brown the finely chopped onion in the pot, add the chopped fennel and a little water and boil for a few minutes. Pour the tomato pulp diluted in water and add salt and pepper. Bring to the boil and add the boiled beans. Simmer till the sauce thickens.

-A cretan mountaineer transports his agricultural products in..."the traditional way".
-Carefree hours in a cretan café around 1920.
-Cretan family in the beginning of 20th century.

CRETAN TRADITIONAL BREAD

It is a saying in Crete that: "food is the yarn in the stomach and bread is the shuttle". And indeed bread has always been extremely important to Cretans. Sometimes the word "bread" implies the whole meal: "-Come and eat bread with us" is an invitation to lunch. No meal can be conceived without it. There has always been a great variety of breads, according to the season and according to the different feasts, adding to the general enjoyment of the meals.

This love of bread is nothing new: first-rate cereals were cultivated in the plains of the island and on the terraces of the mountainous regions way back in Antiquity and Minoans stored large amounts of cereals in the warehouses of their palaces.

Bread played a very specific role in every day life in Ancient Greece: the flour was kneaded with water, or with water and honey, sometimes with oil or with a special drink made of honey and vinegar or wine. The variety of breads in Ancient Greece was really impressive: it had to do with the kind of flour used (barley or wheat), the dough, the manner of cooking it and the shape. The main types of cooking bread were the following:

-bread baked in the oven ("**klivanitis**" from "klivanos" which means oven)

-a thin bread cooked on the spit ("**escharitis"** from "schara", the spit)

-bread cooked in a bain Marie (**"plytos**" from "pleo", to float)

-bread cooked on coals ("**apopyrias**" from "pyr", fire)

-bread basted in oil ("**alifalitis**" from "alifo", to baste)

The variety in shape was even greater: rectangular, round, semi-circular, flat.

During the Middle-Ages, in Crete, there was again a great variety of bread, according to the dough (with water, honey or milk), and the manner of baking. "Bread", too, was a generic word, meaning simply food.

Country oven in the region of Ierapetra.

In more recent years the varieties of bread have evolved from the every day life of the inhabitants of the island. Bread was made of barley, wheat or both,

"Eftazymo"

An old photo with a cretan couple in their traditional costumes

The Christmas bread on the Christmas table ("Christopsomo")

sometimes baked into rusks; there were the sacred breads as well and other specific kinds of bread which present a particular interest. The custom of preparing sacred breads for rituals goes back to Minoan times; this is shown on one of the sarcophagi found in Ayia Triada in the region of Mesara: a basket of bread is represented next to a bird and beside the famous sacred tree of the Minoans. These are the gifts offered to the gods: the seeds of the new crop. Exactly the same custom is still to be seen nowadays in all the Greek world: the faithful regularly take a special kind of bread to church to be blessed. In both cases, then and now, the bread is a bloodless offering to the divinity. The more common of these sacred breads were called "popona", small round breads kneaded in a special fashion. Aristophanes mentions them:

"After this, he walked round the altars, on which lay the "popona"
(Plato, 678-680).

Several genuine Ancient Greek customs related to sacred breads survived in Crete right up to the middle of our century. Minoans, as we said before, offered the first breads of the new year to the gods. The Greeks of the classic period offered their gods a bread called "thalisio" or "thargilio", again the first one made with the cereals of the new crop. Until recently this practice was still common in many parts of Crete.

Consecrated breads.

Different kinds of bread were, and still are, baked according to the time of year and according to the feasts: Christmas breads ("Christopsoma"), other breads called "Lazari", the "Lambrokouloures" at Easter, the "Fanouropites" on the feast day of Saint Fanourios and so on. Each region has its own way of preparing and shaping these breads. The decoration of the breads used to be of great importance and in some villages there are still old women called "xobliastres" who specialise in the decoration of breads, showing great experience and talent. In the village of Platanias in Chania, special bread rolls are baked on the feast of the local saint, Ayios Dimitris, and are known as Ayiodimitriatika or Dimitrokouloura. Other breads of special interest are the ritual ones: "artos" and "prosfora"(from "prosfero", to offer) with their special seal, breads for baptisms, for engagements, for weddings, the bridegroom's bread, the best man's bread, the bread for the guests and so on. All these breads were particular to each region and the decoration, figurative and symbolic, was often a masterpiece. Other breads, apart from the daily bread and the sacred ones, are the "moustokouloura", the "paximadia" (rusks), the "stafidopsoma"(with raisins), the "koulouria" (rolls) and many more.

Very ancient customs of a definite folkloric interest have reached us through the centuries: they refer to the planting of the cereals, the crops, the threshing, the milling and, finally, the making of the bread.

The Christmas bread

("Christopsomo")

This used to be the main feature of the Christmas table, in the countryside in Crete. Beautifully decorated, all golden, it occupied the centre of the table. Its preparation was -still is- something of a ritual: first the leaven, then the lighting of the fire, the kneading, the shaping... especially the shaping! In most parts of the island it had a large cross in its centre, which, if looked at side-ways, shows the letter X, the first letter of the Greek word "Christos", Christ. In other regions, the cross stood above the branches of a tree, also made of dough, on top of the Christmas bread. In different parts of the island it was more or less decorated with partridges, flowers

- Rusks ("Paximadi")
-"Eftazymo"

Toiling the earth (Photo 1900 - 1910)

and so on.

Only the head of the family was allowed to cut this bread: holding the knife like a Minoan priest, he blessed himself, wished all those present (everyone was standing) a Happy Christmas and then cut the bread.

The leaven

You need wheat flour, a little salt, a little warm water.

Make a hole in the middle of the yeast, add the salt and the water and knead. Let the dough stand in a warm place for 4 days until it turns sour. Keep it in the refrigerator until you need it. (see recipes below)

"Christopsomo"

4 kilos of flour
200 grams of yeast
1300 grams of sugar
1 tbsp. of cinnamon
a little mastic
4 small cups of oil
1 small cup of orange juice
1 small cup of "alousia" (water boiled with ashes)
1 small glass of raki and cognac

Prepare the leaven the evening before: take 750 grams of flour, the yeast and a little warm water. Next morning, add 400 grams of sugar, half the oil and a little flour: knead. Leave it to rise and then add the other ingredients. Put a lid on the dough and put it away somewhere warm to rise; later on give it the shape of the "christopsomo". Dab with butter, place a walnut in its centre and bake.

Michalis Bitsakakis, Petrokefali, Mesara.

Bread "paximadi" (rusk)

10 kilos of flour
200 grams of yeast and leaven
5 or 6 glasses of cinnamon juice
a little salt
water or "alousia" (see above recipe: tie some ashes in a clean cloth and boil in water)
1 tbsp. of mastic and "machlepi" (both are strong sweet smelling spices)
sesame seeds

Prepare the leaven the night before using the yeast, a little warm water and a kilo of flour. Next morning mix this leaven with some that has been kept in the refrigerator (see above note on leaven), add the other ingredients and knead thoroughly. (First place the flour and the spices in one corner and the liquid ingredients in the other: as you work the dough, take in the flour bit by bit. You might need to add some water or "alousia"). Leave the dough to rise in a warm place and then fashion long and narrow breads, roll them in sesame seeds which have been sprinkled with a little sugared water, mark the slices with a knife (but don't cut through) and put aside to rise once more. Then bake them either on wood or in the kitchen stove. To make rusks, break off the slices (the same day or later on) and bake again in a moderate oven.

Michalis Bitsakakis, Petrokefali, Mesara.

Easter bread

2 kilos of flour
200 grams of yeast and a little leaven

Traditional baptismal bread with in-laid decorations

5 cups of sugar
8 eggs
3 cups of butter
2 glasses of warm milk
"machlepi" (a strong sweet smelling spice), aniseed, mastic, orange peel

Prepare the leaven with the yeast, 1 lb. of flour and the warm milk. When it rises, mix it with the leaven and the other ingredients

and knead thoroughly. Cover with a lid and put in a warm place to rise. Then fashion the breads, wait till they rise again and bake.

Michalis Bitsakakis, Petrokefali, Mesara.

- Breads with in-laid decorations
-Rusks

Traditional unleavened bread ("eftazymo")

5 kilos of wheat flour
1 kilo of chick peas
a little salt
300 grams sugar
3 litres of water
2 hot peppers
5 or 6 laurel leaves
cinnamon
pepper, aniseed
cumin.

Ground the chick peas and add the

The bread rolls suspended on sticks to be safer. Agricultural economy in Crete of 19th century. "Lychnostatis" museum, Chersonisos.

finely chopped hot peppers, a little salt, a little flour and a little warm water: mix well. Place the covered dough in a warm place- the temperature must remain constant-. It'll take about 7 hours to rise and will have a little froth on top: this is called "kounenos".

Warm some water and add the laurel leaves; mix in the "kounenos", add some flour and knead. When this rises, repeat the operation adding the rest of the flour, the spices and the sugar. Cover the dough, let it rise; then shape the "eftazyma" (several of them). Once these too rise, dab the surface with sugared water and sprinkle with lots of sesame seeds. Bake in a hot oven.

Wedding bread

10 kilos of flour
150 grams of yeast and a little leaven
2 tbsp. of salt
1 bottle of beer
1 and a half cup of oil
1 glass of orange juice
1 kilo of sugar
cinnamon
nutmeg

Prepare the leaven the evening before with 150 grams yeast, a little warm water and 2 kilos of flour. In the morning mix with the leaven that has been kept in the refrigerator, add the other ingredients and as much water (or "alousia", ash-water, see recipes above) as it takes: knead very thoroughly. Cover the dough and let it rise in a warm place. Then fashion the breads, roll them in sesame seeds that have been sprinkled with sugared water and let them rise again. Finally, bake them in a very hot oven.

Chrysoula Mavromanolaki, Galia, Mires.

Cretan sacred bread (Arti)

leaven
4 kilos of flour
1 glass of wine
1 cup of oil
1 kilo of sugar
1 tbsp. of salt
2 or 3 grains of mastic
pepper
water
3 or 4 laurel leaves

The night before take the leaven you have in the refrigerator, add a little warm water and knead with some flour.

Boil the water with the laurel leaves and when it cools add a little to the leaven. Knead constantly while you add the other ingredients, and, very slowly, the flour. Let this rise in a warm place and then fashion the breads: shape two balls, place one on top of the other and press them down with the special seal for sacred breads. Put these breads in oiled baking tins, let them rise once again and then bake them in a moderate oven.

Eleni Simitzi, Rethimnon.

The ploughing in the byzantine times, 11th century.

PASTA

The word "macarounes" is to be found in Cretan texts of the Middle-Ages and many believe it to be the same word as "macaronia" which today means pasta.

This was a very common food in Crete during the Turkish occupation. The different ways of preparing pasta show an experience that has reached us through the centuries. Usually pasta was made a little before being cooked, but many Cretan housewives found ways of drying it out in the air (never in the sun) so as to store it and it was cooked weeks, sometimes months, later.

Meals based on starch (or dough) were easy and quick to prepare: especially for the cold winter evenings pasta was a light and wholesome meal mainly for the inhabitants of the countryside. Among the better known Cretan kinds of pasta are the "manghiri" of Eastern Crete, "chilofta", lasagne, "skioufichta macarounia" and "chilobazina" .

The rolling out of the pastry sheet and the preparation of "manghiri".

"Manghiri"

(for 5 persons)

Ingredients:

1 glass of water
1 lb. of wheat flour
1 small cup of oil
salt
1 cup of oil for frying
grated "anthotiro" (hard white cheese)

This was a unique Cretan dish, usually served in the evening and in the countryside. Easy to prepare, it was very popular, especially during Lent.

Prepare a dough with the water, the flour and the salt. Let it stand for about an hour and then roll it out. First cut the thin dough in strips one cm. wide and then in long and narrow pieces. Roll them in flour so they won't stick and boil half of them in 2 litres of salted water. Brown the other half in oil and them empty them, with the oil, in the pot with the boiled ones: stir and serve hot with grated "anthotiro".

Loula Metaxa, Heraklion.

"Manghiri"

"Makarounia skioufichta"

(for 5 persons)
1 lb. of wheat flour
1 glass of water
1 cup of fresh goat's butter ("staka")
a little lemon juice, salt
grated "anthotiro"(see above)

Make a dough with the flour, the water, the salt and the lemon juice. Let it stand for an hour and then fashion the pasta: shape a string of pasta the width of a finger and cut off a piece of about 3 cms. long with your 2 fingers; press the fingers hard into the dough and rubbing them against the table separate with skilful movements so as to shape short and thick macaroni (hollow in the middle). Spread the macaroni on some flour to dry for an hour or so. Then boil them in water for half an hour. Take them out of the pot and on to a dish and serve hot with grated "anthotiro".

Loula Metaxa, Heraklion.

"Chilos" or "Chilofta"

A very common pasta dish, easy to prepare and therefore often made in winter when the family returned home exhausted from the fields at sunset having gathered olives all day long. In some places this dish was known simply as "chilos", as in the Lent saying: "Forty days, forty chiloudies", that is, during the forty days of Lent one ate "chilos" forty times.

Often, to avoid having to prepare the dough every time, the "chilofta" were dried and stored and could thus be cooked at a moment's notice just like today's pasta.

"Chilofta"

Prepare the dough with a certain amount of wheat flour, water and salt: the result must be on the hard side. Roll out the paste and once it's dry cut out long strips and then in long narrow pieces about half a cm wide, or less. You can also roll the paste around the rolling pin and thus cut it all the way down in a long strip, as for "manghiri": this makes it easier to cut narrower strips of up to 5cms wide and then with a knife cut more long and narrow pieces. Boil in salted water until cooked and serve in a dish with grated cheese ("kefalotiri" or "galotiri", both Cretan cheeses) and lots of very hot butter. Instead of grated cheese, you can melt some "mizithra" (white soft cheese) when boiling the "chilos" and at the end pour this over the dish so as to obtain a kind of soup.

Eleni Anipsitaki-Daouraki, Sitia.

"Chilofta" with milk

Proceed as above but instead of using water for the boiling, use milk. Take care it doesn't boil over. You can also add sugar and less salt, if you want it sweet.

To be served as a soup: a thin crust forms on the top and many housewives sprinkle this crust with cinnamon.

Eleni Anipsitaki-Daouraki, Sitia.

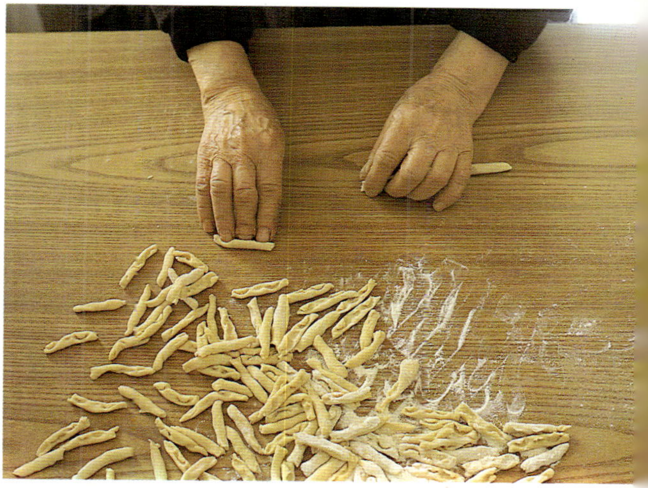

-"Macaronia skioufichta"
-"Macaronia skioufichta"
- "Chilofta"

"Chilofta" with honey

A special dish for women who have just given birth. It was believed to give the mother strength and that it was good for her milk. Boil the "chilofta" as above, in water. Use some of this water to dilute some honey, pour this over the "chilofta" and sprinkle with a little cinnamon.

Eleni Anipsitaki-Daouraki, Sitia.

Lasagne

The "elegant" macaroni in the old days.

A dish known during the Venetian occupation. Lasagne were short, wide and with an opening in the middle. Later on lasagne were made with grain flour. The paste was made with flour, milk, eggs and butter and then rolled out.

The hand-mill (photo by Andreas Theodorakis)

Xinochontros

To prepare traditional Cretan lasagne, you must cut the rolled out paste in small triangles (not more than 5 or 6 cms on its longest side) which you twist round the spindle to give them the shape of a cone. In some parts of the island they used to cut rectangular pieces, twisting the two opposite corners on the spindle.

Like for "skioufichta" macaroni, there are many ways of cooking them; the most common one was cooking them in the broth where chicken or goat had been boiled. As we said before lasagne were served on more formal occasions, often during Carnival and, in some regions, at Christmas.

Macaroni served at weddings

(makaronia tou gamou)

First boil 1 kilo goat meat, then take it out of the pot, add some water and some salt and in this boil the macaroni. Serve in plates with grated cheese ("anthotiro", cretan hard white cheese).

Maria Kallergi, Anoyia.

The ready-made pasta found nowadays can be cooked in all these ways. The most common way of cooking pasta in the last decades is according to the wedding recipe: the famous Cretan macaroni boiled in meat broth, ideally goat, which is usually served on grand occasions with the macaroni.

THE HANDMILL
("chiromilos")

Every house had a stone hand-worked mill in Crete. Used for the preparation of many meals, it was an indispensable tool in every household in the countryside. Whenever she ran out of bread, the Cretan housewife could quickly grind some wheat without having to go to the windmill; in this manner she could also bake the famous pie called "chiromilopita". (see chapter on the traditional Cretan bread).

The handmill is made of two large round chiselled stones, the male stone and the female stone. The heavier bottom stone has a diameter of about half a meter and remains still when the handmill is in use. The stone is chiselled with care to form a cavity in the middle and its sides are 10 to 20 cms high, according to the stone. Somewhere along the side there is a spout to let the ground cereal out. In the middle a good sturdy "catch" (usually wooden, sometimes metal) holds the top stone in place.

The top stone is slighter and in its middle has a big enough hole for the "catch" around which it turns. It has a wooden handle on its side to make it turn.

Below you will find recipes which usually require the use of the handmill, but since this is not such a common tool you can buy roughly ground wheat in the market, or you can use an electric grinder.

"Xinochondros"

This is one of the most common foods of Crete. It is made of ground wheat and sour milk and can be eaten either fresh or after it has dried in the sun (in some villages in Amari and in Ayios Vassilis in Rethimnon they prefer drying it in the shade). This isn't such an easy affair because cats love eating the "xinochondros" so often it is placed on a plank hung in mid-air, where the cats can't reach it.

The ingredients:

3 kilos of fresh milk (sheep's or goat's milk)

1 kilo of wheat

salt.

Leave the milk out of the refrigerator for three days to go sour. Grind the wheat, but roughly, not to the point of flour. In the old days the handmill was used for this operation. Boil the milk, add the wheat and stir till it thickens. Once it cools, take the mixture out with a spoon and spread it on a floured tin or on clean kitchen towels. If you want to store the "xinochondros" place the tin or the towels out in the sun to dry it, turning the pieces around every day. Store in clean cotton sacks.

Adriana Markoutsaki, Kapsodasos, Sfakia.

Transport of the cereals.

"Xinochondros" soup with goat

(for 5-6 persons)
1 plate of "xinochondros"
1 kilo of goat meat
salt,pepper.

Boil the meat. Take the meat out of the pot, strain the broth and add more water to make a soup (not so thick). When it comes to the boil, add the "xinochondros" and simmer till cooked.

Eupr. Psillaki, Kastamonitsa, Heraklion.

"Chondros"

Wheat that has been ground in the handmill. It was very widely used in Cretan cooking, and is especially good with snails. Equally good were the "dolmades" stuffed with "chondros".

The main difference between "chondros" and "xinochondros" is that one is just wheat while the other, as we saw above, is prepared with sour milk.

Often "chondros" was used instead of rice (like in "dolmades"), either in mountainous regions where no rice was produced, or else because there was no rice to be found in the local market.

"Chondros with leaks

Clean a kilo of leaks, chop and brown them in a cup of oil. Add 1 lb of chopped ripe tomatoes and simmer for about 20 minutes. Pour 5 glasses of water in the pot and, when it comes to the boil, add half a kilo of "chondros", salt and pepper. Simmer until cooked, but towards the end you have to stir often.

Pork with "chondros"

1 kilo of pork with its fat
1 onion
1 small cup of oil

juice of 1 lemon
1 small cup of vinegar
half a kilo of "chondros"
salt, pepper.

Brown the pork and the onion in very little oil. When the pork is nicely browned pour the lemon juice and the vinegar and then about 5 cups of water. When it comes to the boil, add the "chondros", salt and pepper and simmer till cooked, stirring often.

Athina Epanomeritaki, Heraklion.

Preparing "kallitsounia" and "mizithropites"

"KALLITSOUNIA" AND "MIZITHROPITES"

All food (main dish or sweet) based on "mizithra"(a white soft cheese which can be sweet and saltless or sour) is very popular in Crete. Mizithra is the second product in the cheese-making process and is made after the "malaka", on a very gentle fire. When the mizithra takes form in the bottom of the pot, it is removed and placed in special baskets, taking their shape. "Kallitsounia", considered more of a dessert, were formerly part of every feast: Easter was incomplete without them and, in most parts of the island, they were made on Holy Thursday morning, right after church. These "kallitsounia" were usually square and large and were baked in an oven heated with wood which gave them a very special taste. During Carnival too there were a lot of "kallitsounia" everywhere on the island, though "mizithropites", which were fried, were more common.

There is a great variety of both. The wonderful creativity of Cretan housewives found expression in the many ways of preparing these cheese pies: they differ not only in the preparation itself and in the cooking, but in the shape of the final product. "Kallitsounia" are usually round with a sort of a crown and are called "lychnarakia" (oil lamps) because of their shape; they can also be square and double, or triangular and double. "Mizithropites" on the other hand are usually semicircular, whether large or small. Aesthetics played as important a role as the taste and, thanks to the imagination of Cretan women, the result in Cretan cheese pies is as pretty as it is savoury.

There's no one single way of preparing

cheese pies in Crete: in Sitia, for example, they make "anevata kallitsounia", seemingly in character with the gentle disposition of the inhabitants; in Ierapetra they make "nerates mizithropites" and in central Crete, "agnopites"; in Anoyia and the mountainous region of Milopotamos the "mizithropites" are known as "sarikopites" from the "sariki" - the traditional head-dress Cretan men use to wear. The "sfakianopites" from Sfakia are fried without oil, the ones in Chania have no sugar etc.

Easter "kallitsounia"

1 cup of fine olive oil
1 cup of butter or milk cream
1 cup of milk
1 cup of sugar
1 teasp. of baking powder diluted in a little lemon juice
flour, as much as needed for a soft dough

For the stuffing:

"Kallitsounia"

"Kallitsounia"
-"Lychnarakia" (small oil lamps)

a kilo and a half of "mizithra",
1 or
2 eggs,
10 tbsps of sugar,
cinnamon and finely chopped mint.

Prepare the dough, cover it and set it aside to rise. Then roll out the dough and cut out circular pieces which you fill with 1 tbsp. of the stuffing each and then you shape them in the manner of small oil lamps: twisting the edge all around, like a crown. Dab with egg and sprinkle with cinnamon. Bake till golden.

Titika Saklabani, Heraklion.

"Kallitsounia" from Chania with leaven

The **dough**:
3 kilos of flour
1 and a half cup of butter
1 cup of oil
2 glasses of milk, 2 eggs
a little crushed coriander

"Kallitsounia"

a little crushed mastic

1 glass and a half of "alousia"(water in which some ashes, tied in a clean cloth, have been boiled), leaven

The **stuffing:** 4 kilos of mizithra, 3 or 4 eggs, a little finely chopped mint.

Leave the following mixture to rise overnight: the leaven with a glass of "alousia" and 1 kilo of flour. Next morning, beat the oil with the butter in half a glass of "alousia" and add this to the leaven. Mix and add the milk and the egg and go on working the dough adding the rest of the flour little by little and the other ingredients. Then let the dough rest for a while.

Roll out the dough and proceed to cut out round pieces with a saucer and to stuff them with the stuffing just as for the "anevata kallitsounia" of the preceding recipe. When they have risen, dab them with egg, sprinkle the sesame seeds over them and bake.

Katerina Papadaki, Chania.

Fried "kallitsounia" from Heraklion

The **dough:**
1 kilo of flour
2 eggs
half a cup of oil
a few drops of lemon juice
1 teasp. of baking soda
1 glass of milk
some salt

The **stuffing:**
1 lb. of sour "mizithra"
1 lb. of sweet "mizithra"
2 eggs
1 cup of sugar
a little finely chopped mint
1 tbsp. of cinnamon

"Kallitsounia anevata" from Sitia

Mix the oil with the lemon. Add the beaten eggs and the milk; mix again. Work in the flour mixed with the baking soda. Put the dough aside until you have prepared the stuffing mixing all the ingredients.

Roll out the dough and proceed as above to shape the "kallitsounia" like crescents pressing the sides with the help of a fork.

Deep-fry and serve either with honey or sugar.

"Anevata kallitsounia" from Sitia

2 kilos of flour
3 cups of olive oil
6 eggs
2 glasses of sugar
50 grams of beer yeast (leaven was used of old)
1 cup of milk

For the **stuffing:** 2 kilos of sweet mizithra, 2 egg yolks, 1 cup of sugar and cinnamon.

Dissolve the yeast in the warm milk, add a little flour and let the leaven rise. Put the oil in another bowl and amalgamate it with the sugar. Add the beaten eggs and the leaven. Make a dough adding the rest of the flour. Let it rest until you get the stuffing ready; then roll out the dough and in sheets half a cm thick cut out round pieces with the help of a saucer. In the middle of each piece place a tbsp. of the stuffing. Since the "anevata kallitsounia" are usually square, fold each time the two opposite sides of the dough. Put the cheese cakes aside for a couple of hours to rise; then brush them with a mixture of egg beaten with a few drops of lemon, sprinkle some sesame seeds over them and bake until golden.

Eleni Anipsitaki-Daouraki, Sitia.

Fried "kallitsounia" from Chania

1.5 kilo of flour
a little salt
juice of 1 lemon
a small cup of oil
water (about 2 glasses)

The stuffing:
1 lb of "mizithra"
1 lb. of "anthotyro" (dry and hard mizithra)
1 lb. of "malaka" (the first result in the cheese-making operation)
3 eggs

Prepare a dough with the flour, the oil, the salt, the lemon juice and the water.

In another bowl mix all the different cheeses with the eggs.

Roll out the dough, cut out round pieces with a saucer, put some stuffing on each piece, fold and press down the sides carefully; now deep-fry and serve with or without honey, as you like.

Katerina Papadaki, Chania.

«Kallitsounia» from Rethymnon with yeast

the dough:
2 glasses of milk
2 or 3 eggs
a little salt
50 grams yeast or leaven
half a glass of orange juice
1 kilo of flour

the filling:
1 kilo of sweet "mizithra" cheese
200 grams of feta cheese
1 egg
mint

Dissolve the yeast in warm milk, add the salt, the beaten eggs, the orange juice and the flour. Knead the dough which should be very light.

Prepare the filling with both kinds of cheese, the egg and the mint.

Heat some oil in a pan. Have a cup of oil handy to oil your fingers every time you take a small ball of dough, so it won't stick. Press this ball down a little to place some filling in it, re-shaping the ball so as to close it. Flatten it out and fry it on both sides. Repeat this operation until you use up all the dough and the filling.

(You can use the same dough to make turkey or chicken pies)

Victoria Athanasiadou, Chania.

"Kallitsounia" from Rethymnon

«Sfakianopites» (cheese pasties from Sfakia)

In Sfakia cheese pies are prepared quite differently and this is due to the rather different kind of life in that region. Most inhabitants still were until recently stock-raisers and so their food had to be dry enough to be carried up into the mountains. Sauces were out of the question in the White Mountains (Madara). The frugal food, almost Doric in its simplicity, was particularly savoury and was based on the local dairy production.

Ingredients for 10 "sfakianopites":
10 tbsps of flour
10 tbsps of "mizithra"
a small cup of olive oil, salt, and as much water as needed.

Prepare a soft dough with the flour, the water, the oil and some salt. Roll it out and prepare 10 separate pieces the size of a small saucer. Shape 10 small balls with the cheese and put one ball on each piece of dough pulling at the sides so as to cover the cheese. Press this down again with the pin so that each ball is the size of a small saucer. Fry in a pan without oil turning them upside down constantly so they won't burn. Pour honey over each one before serving.

Evangelia Katsanevaki, Askyfou, Sfakia.

The cheese pies from Sfakia are famous, both because of the excellent quality of their ingredients and because of the way they are prepared. Professor Michael Defner travelled in Crete in 1919 and having tried the cheese pies from Sfakia, wrote enthusiastically: "O, my God, what relish! No king in the wide world has ever eaten a better pie. I must have had six or more and the others didn't lag behind!" (Defner, A traveller's impressions of Western Crete, page 147).

"Tiropita" or Cheese pie

1 lb. of "filo"(paper-thin pastry that can be bought ready for use)
2 glasses of milk

"Sfakianopιtes":

3 tbsps of flour
2 tbsps. of butter
5 or 6 eggs
400 grams cheese (preferably parmesan)

Prepare a thick sauce with the butter, the flour and the milk. Add the beaten eggs and the cheese.

Place 5 or 6 sheets of buttered "filo" on the bottom of a baking tin and spread the stuffing over it. Cover with 4 or 5 buttered sheets of "filo" which you sprinkle with some water. Bake until golden.

Anna Katsoulogiorgi, Heraklion.

Cheese pasties

(Tiropitakia)

2 cups of butter
1 cup of oil
1 kilo of flcur
milk
salt
2 tbsps of baking powder
400 grams of cheese (the "kaseri" kind)

Prepare a dough with the butter, the oil, a little salt, the baking powder, the flour and as

much milk as it will take. Grate the cheese and add it to the dough. Roll out the dough, cut out round pieces,brush them with egg and bake.

"Agnopites"

Prepare a normal dough with half a kilo of flour, a small cup of oil, 1 glass of water, salt and a little lemon juice. Separate into small balls, the size of mandarines. Open a small hole in the middle of each ball and fill with a teasp. of "mizithra" which has been softened with a little water or milk. Pull the dough over to cover the hole; press down these balls and roll them out with the rolling pin to give them the size and shape of a saucer. Deep-fry them and serve with honey, grape-juice syrup or sugar.

Eupr. Psillaki, Kastamonitsa,
Heraklion.

"Sarikopites"

Prepare the dough as above. Roll out the dough and cut it in strips 8 to 10 cms wide and 25 to 30 cms long. Spread the sour "mizithra" all along the strips, and fold them. Starting at one end, twist the ribbon in a spiral. The shape is similar to a "sariki" (the traditional head-dress of Cretan men which is why the pies are called "sarikopites"). Deep-fry and serve with honey, grape-juice syrup or sugar.

Eleni Bitsakaki, Petrokefali.

- Fried "kallitsounia" from Heraklion
-Pies with mizithra cheese
-"Boureki"
-"Sarikopites"

The market of Heraklion around 1950.

«Mizithropites» or cottage cheese pasties

Prepare a usual dough with 1 kilo of flour, 2 tbsps of oil, a little salt, 2 glasses of water and a small glass of raki to make a fluffy dough.

Roll out the dough, cut out round pieces and place some "mizithra" (sweet or sour, whichever you like) on each half, folding the other half over it and forming crescents. Deep-fry.

«Boureki»

The dough:
1 small cup of oil
1 teasp. of salt
1 glass of water
the juice of 1 lemon
1 lb. of flour
the filling:
1 kilo and a half of sweet "mizithra" cheese
1 cup of sugar
2 tbsps of cinnamon
2 eggs
1 tbsp. of grated lemon peel.

Knead the dough, roll it out and place one third of it on the bottom of a buttered baking tin. Sprinkle with a little sugar and cinnamon and put the tin in a pre-heated oven for 10 minutes to stiffen the dough a

Transport of grapes in Crete around 1950.

little. On top of this, place a layer of cheese, then another third of the dough, again sprinkling some sugar and cinnamon, then the second half of the cheese. Place the last third of the dough over this cheese layer, sprinkling it with sugar and cinnamon and pour 2 or 3 tbsps of butter over it all before baking. Half way through the baking, pour a glass of milk over the "boureki".

Maria Bitsakaki, Heraklion.

"Mizithroboureko"

(large "mizithra" pastry)

400 grams of crumbled sour "mizithra"
250 grams of sweet "mizithra"
3 or 4 eggs
4 tbsps of sugar
cinnamon
1 lb. of ready made "filo"(paper-thin pastry)

The syrup:
3 cups of sugar
2 cups of water
the juice of half a lemon

Work the sweet "mizithra" with the sour one and with the eggs, the sugar and the cinnamon.

Place half the sheets of pastry ("filo") in a buttered pan, buttering each sheet. Spread the cheese mixture on top and cover with the rest of the buttered "filo". Lightly cut the surface with a knife to mark the individual serving portions; sprinkle with a little water and bake in a moderate oven till golden. Then take it out of the oven, let it cool and sprinkle generously with the syrup you have prepared in the meantime.

Titika Saklabani, Heraklion

The pie-boy. Crete, beginning of the century.

SWEETS

A peculiar sort of Cretan sweet made with flour, **"plakounda",** was already famous in Ancient Greece: the preparation of these "plakoundes" was rather special and had to do with the ingredients used, the shape given them and in general the aesthetic of the time: to make them more attractive the cakes were decorated in geometric style and sometimes the dough was placed in specially designed moulds to acquire the desired form and then they were baked.

Other well-known sweets were called **"flepsia",** made with flour, honey and milk; **"itria",** made with boiled wheat or with sesame seeds and honey; and later on a kind called "**pemmata**", with honey and **"sousamides"** reminiscent of today's "**pastelli**". In Ancient Crete **"tiganies"** or **"tiganites"** were exactly the same as the ones that are so popular nowadays on the island, made, then as now, with flour and water and fried in very hot olive oil, served covered in honey or grape-juice syrup. The basic way of preparing sweets hasn't changed through the centuries, as is shown in different studies: Minoans used a lot of honey, sesame seeds and saffron. In classic years another famous Cretan sweetmeat was the "glykinas" which was made with sweet wine and oil, as we learn from Athenaeus in his book *The Deipnosophists (XIV,53,645D).* This author also mentions the "gastrin" *(The Deipnosophists XIV,57,647-648F)*, yet another Cretan sweet made with walnuts, almonds, poppy seeds and honey: this sweet was enrobed in ground sesame seeds, something like the "baklava" we know nowadays and there is strong reason to believe that remote descendants of "gastrin" are to be found in Eastern Crete and are called "patouda".

In Venetian times the most common sweet in Crete was "pastelli", the Byzantine "pastillos". But this "pastelli" was different from the ones that are prepared nowadays with honey and sesame seeds: most certainly the Byzantines and the Cretans of the Middle-Ages called "pastelli" a sweet made with must and flour, similar to "moustalevria" a very well known sweet in modern Crete ("moustos" is must and "alevri" is flour) which is dried out in the sun. In eastern Crete "moustalevria" is cut in triangles or squares and these pieces are called "kiofteria". The word "pastelli" is not used in Crete to describe the famous sesame-and-honey cakes, it rather implies figs dried in the sun.

The sesame cake famous since Byzantine years was called "sisamaton" or "sisamitis".

In modern Crete honey and grape-juice syrup still continue to form the basis of all sweets and the other ingredients are all of local produce: the flour, the sesame seeds, the walnuts, the almonds, and many dairy products, like "mizithra". A number of old recipes have remained basically unchanged, though they have been adapted to new conditions and new needs.

The sweets based on "mizithra" have very old roots as well; unfortunately there aren't any sources whereby we can compare how the housewives of the Middle-Ages and the housewives of the 20th century used the same ingredients, quite possibly in the same quantities. What were known as "tetiromeni plakoundes" *(Artemidoros in Oneirokr.1,72)* must have been something like modern sweet Cretan "kallitsounia".

In the recipe notebooks of the 19th century that we were able to consult, the western influence was beginning to be felt in the preparation of sweets: but this was only the case

A variety of preserves

Fig sweet

in town families that were well-off and who in any case knew the local recipes perfectly well. This was the time when the famous sweets called "glyka tou koutaliou" were at their height (literally, sweets of the spoon, referring to the fruit preserves served in very small quantities: pear, cherry, grape and quince are among the large variety of "glyka tou koutaliou"). There was a noticeable effort in the 19th century to use local fruit in the preparation of sweets.

Cherry (kerasi) sweet

1 kilo of cherries
1 kilo of sugar
2 glasses of water
the juice of one lemon

Take out the cherry stones with a pip-remover. Put the water, sugar and cherries in the pot and boil for ten minutes. Let the mixture stand for 24 hours and then boil it again until it amalgamates. Add the lemon juice, bring to the boil and the preserve is ready.

Maria Xiroudaki-Thalassinou

Sour cherry (vysino) sweet

As above.

Strawberry (fraoula) sweet

1 kilo of sugar
1 kilo of strawberries
1 glass of water
the juice of 2-3 lemons

Wash the not-too ripe strawberries and put them to dry on a clean kitchen towel. Remove the stalks, place the fruit in an earthenware pot, pour over it the juice of the lemons and the sugar and let it stand for 12 hours. Then transfer into a pot, add the water and boil for 5 minutes. Let the strawberries stand again for 24 hours and then boil for another 5 minutes. Take the pot from the fire, let the mixture cool off and, with great care, put the strawberries on to a plate. Boil the syrup again and when it binds return the fruit to the pot. The preserve is ready: when cold enough put it in a jar.

+Chrisi Prevelaki, Rethimnon.

Apricot (Verykoko) sweet

1 kilo of not too ripe apricots
1 kilo of sugar, 2 cups of water
juice of 1 lemon

Remove the stones and put the apricots in lime-water for one hour. Rinse them carefully and drain them.

Prepare the syrup with the water and the sugar and add the fruit. Boil till the preserve binds and near the end add the lemon juice.

+Eleni Anemoyanni, Heraklion.

Orange preserve

Orange (portokali) sweet

6 or 7 oranges, of the kind with the thick peel
1 kilo and a half of sugar
3 glasses of water
vanilla essence
the juice of 1 lemon

Grate the orange peel very finely, wash the oranges and boil them whole until they become soft. Drain them and cut each orange in 8 slices. Remove the tougher parts with a pair of scissors. Prepare the syrup with the water and the sugar and then plunge the orange pieces in this syrup, boiling constantly until they bind. Add the vanilla essence and the lemon juice and after a few minutes remove from the fire.

One can also make an orange sweet using only the orange peel: rub it clean, cut each orange peel into 6 pieces that you roll up and then tie to each other with a thread; boil them, bind them with the syrup and take away the thread.

In the same manner you can prepare preserves of **sour orange**, **citron**, **bergamot** and other fruits taking care to boil them first, then cut them and then leave them in cold water(which you have to change) for 1 or 2 days to get rid of the bitterness.

Titika Saklabani, Heraklion.

Mandarine (mandarini) marmalade

1 lb. of mandarines
1 kilo of sugar
1 glass of water

the juice of half a lemon

Boil and mash the mandarines. Add the water and the sugar until the syrup binds. At the end, add the lemon juice and remove the pot from the fire.

Titika Saklabani, Heraklion.

Fig (syko) sweet

1 kg fresh green figs
1 kg of sugar
1 glass of water
the juice of 1 lemon

Boil the figs and drain them carefully. Boil the water with the sugar for 5 minutes and add the figs. Remove the pot from the fire and leave the figs in the syrup for 24 hours. Then simmer till the syrup binds. Finally add the lemon juice.

†Eleni Anemoyanni, Heraklion.

Quince sweet

(Kydoni gliko)

1 kilo of quinces
1 kilo of sugar
3 glasses of water
200 grams of almonds (optional)
amberosa (aromatic plant used fresh)
the juice of 1 lemon

Peel the quinces and cut them into fine slices. Prepare the syrup by boiling the sugar with the water for 10 minutes. Then add the quince pieces and boil constantly until they bind. A few minutes before removing the pot from the fire add the almonds, the amberosa and the lemon juice.

Eleni Sfakianaki, Heraklion.

Walnut (karydi) in syrup

1 kilo of small fresh (green) walnuts
1 kilo and a half of sugar
750 grams of water
1 stick of cinnamon
10 cloves
2 lemons

Rub the walnuts clean and with a nail, for instance, open a hole in them. Cover them in water and boil them until soft changing the water 2 or 3 times and replacing every time with cold water. Drain them and cover them in water once again, in a bowl. For the next 2 days change the water regularly to get rid of the bitterness. Make a syrup with the water and the sugar. Drain the walnuts and put them in the syrup, bring to the boil; then turn off the heat and leave the nuts in the syrup for 24 hours. Next day boil them again for ten minutes and leave them standing once more for 24 hours. The following day, bring to the boil and bind the walnuts with the syrup, adding the cinnamon, the cloves and the lemon juice just before the end.

Maria Bitsakaki, Heraklion.

Quince preserve.

-«Vassilopita» with orange and mandarine

Pear sweet (achladi)

1 kilo of small pears
1 kilo of sugar
2 cups and a half of water
2 lemons, vanilla essence
almonds (as many as the pears).

Clean the pears removing the core with a special knife and put them in a bowl with water and some lemon juice. Drain them and place a bleached almond in each pear. For 5 minutes boil the water with 1 cup of the sugar and then add the pears and boil for another 10 minutes; add the rest of the sugar and boil for 10 minutes more. Remove from the fire and leave the pears in the syrup for 24 hours. Next day boil till they bind, adding the vanilla essence and the lemon juice a little before the end.

Anna Katsoulogiorgi, Heraklion.

and continue boiling, having added the sugar, until the syrup binds. Towards the end add the lemon juice, the vanilla essence and then remove from the fire. When cold, store in a jar.

Efi Varveraki, Heraklion.

Sweet of grapes

(Stafyli)

2 kilos of grapes
1 kilo of sugar
vanilla essence
the juice of 2 lemons
amberosa (aromatic plant used fresh)

Remove the seeds, wash and strain the grapes. Place them in 3 layers in a pot, with sugar in between the layers. Add the lemon juice and let this stand for one day. Next morning, boil for 10 minutes and again let it stand for a whole day. Finally, boil on the last day till the syrup binds and add the vanilla.

Anna Katsoulogiorgi, Heraklion.

New Year's cake

(Vassilopita)

This cake always has a coin (traditionally a golden one) hidden in it: when the head of the family cuts the cake, he gives a slice to each one and the coin brings luck for the whole new year to whoever finds it in his slice. Slices of the cake are also cut for Christ and for Saint Basil whose nameday is on the 1st of January, and for the household as a whole: if the coin is in one of these slices, the good luck is shared by all and sundry. According to the tradition this custom began in the time of the Saint (Basil the Great is one of the Orthodox church's most important saints): the enemy, it is said, was about to attack the city where he lived; in the hopes of avoiding the pillage that would follow, he persuaded all the inhabitants to turn in their gold and jewellery. But in the end the city was not captured and the problem

Carrot (karoto) sweet

1 kilo of carrots
1 kilo of sugar
3 glasses of water
vanilla essence
the juice of 1 lemon

Clean and roughly grate the carrots. Cover them in water and bring to the boil till they are soft. Strain 3 glasses of the water

remained: how to give each one back his due. So the Saint hit on a solution: to bake small breads and in each one hide a coin or a piece of jewellery. When the breads were handed out the miracle happened: each one, in his bread, got back what was his!

Saint Basil's cake with orange juice

(Vasilopita me portokali)

1200 grams of flour
6 cups of sugar
2 cups of butter
1 cup of cognac
8 to 10 eggs
the juice of 8 oranges
1 teasp. of baking soda
2 teasp. of baking powder

Beat the yokes with the sugar and work in the butter. Dissolve the soda in the orange juice and add this. Beat the whites of the eggs; add half the flour, half the cognac with the baking powder and half the whites. When this has amalgamated, work in the second half of all the ingredients. Empty the cake into a buttered tin and bake.

+Eleni Anemoyanni, Heraklion.

"Synnefiasmeno" (the clouded one)

1 cup of butter
3 cups of sugar
6 eggs
1 cup of milk
2 teasps of baking powder
1 small glass of cognac
4 cups of flour
2 cups of grated chocolate

Mix thoroughly the butter with the sugar and add the beaten yolks.

Work in the baking powder diluted in the cognac and alternate the milk with the flour. Finally add the beaten whites and separate the paste in two: add the grated chocolate to one half. Butter a baking tin and spread one spoonful of the mixture with chocolate, one of the other, alternatively.

Bake for one hour.

+Chrisi Prevelaki, Rethimnon.

"Revani"

1 lb. of yoghurt
1 lb. of rough semolina
1 tbsp. of baking soda
1 cup of sugar
vanilla essence

Apple pie

The **syrup**: 2 cups of sugar
2 cups of water

Dissolve the soda in the yoghurt. Add the sugar, the vanilla and the semolina: mix thoroughly. Bake in a moderate oven. When it has cooled down, pour the syrup over it.

Ketty Lekka, Heraklion.

Apple pie

(Milopita)

5 apples cut in dice
1 grated pear and 1 grated quince
1 cup of oil or butter
2 cups of sugar
5 eggs
1 teasp. of baking soda diluted in the juice of 1 lemon
1 small glass of cognac
1 small bag of baking powder
1 tbsp. of ground cinnamon and clove
3 cups of flour

First beat the butter or the oil with the sugar, then add the beaten yolks, the soda and lemon juice, the cognac with the baking powder, the beaten whites of the eggs, the fruit and the flour. When thoroughly mixed, pour in a baking tin and bake for an hour and a half. If desired, sprinkle with caster sugar before serving.

Efi Varveraki, Heraklion.

Sweet with apples

Glykisma me mila)

Peel and cut nice fresh apples in slices. Spread some apricot jam on each slice and stick by twos. Cover the bottom of a deep baking pan with crumbled biscuits or crumbled small buns and on top place the pairs of apple slices on 2 or 3 layers. Pour 2 glasses of milk over this and 2 or 3 tbsps of sugar. Bake.

+Eleni Anemoyanni, Heraklion.

Cake with dried fruit

1 cup of butter
5 eggs
2 tbsps of ground cinnamon and clove
1 tbsp. of cocoa
1 tbsp. of baking soda
1 tbsp. of baking powder
1 lb. of flour
2 cups of dried fruit(prunes, apricots, dates), which have been macerated in a little cognac and 1 cup of cherry syrup.

The cream:
1 small bag of corn flour
3 cups of milk
2 tbsps of sugar, 1 tbsp. of butter

Beat the butter with the yolks, then add all the other ingredients, mixing in the flour with the soda and the baking powder and finally the fruit. Bake in a moderate oven for about 2 hours.

Prepare the cream and pour it over the cake, sprinkle with some grated coconut.

Efi Varveraki, Heraklion.

"Stafidopita" (pie with raisins)

3 cups of oil
4 cups of sugar
1 and a half tbsp. of ground cinnamon and clove
1 tbsp. of cocoa
2 glasses of water
1 small glass of orange and lemon juice
half a small glass of raki
2 teasps of baking soda
4 cups of raisins
a handful of walnuts
1 kilo of flour
1 glass and a half of cognac

Start mixing the oil with the sugar and then add all the other ingredients one by one (except for the cognac), working the mixture as you go along. Bake in a moderate oven.

When you take the cake out of the oven, pour the cognac over it and let it stand for 12 hours, covered. Finally, turn it upside down, cut it in three parts and keep it well wrapped up in tin foil. To be served in thin slices.

Efi Varveraki, Heraklion.

Walnut cake

(Karydopita)

5 eggs, 1 cup of sugar
1 small glass of cognac or raki
1 teasp. of baking powder
some grated lemon peel
1 tbsp. of ground cinnamon and one of clove
2 cups of fine semolina
1 cup of roughly chopped walnuts

The syrup:
2 cups of sugar
1 cup of water
1 lemon peel
1 stick of cinnamon

Walnut cake

Beat the whites of the eggs stiff and add the sugar. Then add the beaten yolks, the baking powder dissolved in the cognac, the lemon peel, the ground clove and cinnamon, the semolina and the walnuts. Bake in a moderate oven for about one hour and after the cake has cooled down a bit, add the warm syrup.

Anna Katsouloyorgi, Heraklion.

Almond cake with cream

(Amigdalopita me krema)

The "pandespani":
1 cup of butter
2 cups of sugar
4 eggs
1 glass of milk
1 small bag of baking powder
2 cups of flour
1 cup of grated almond

The syrup:
3 cups of sugar
1 glass of water
1 glass of mandarine juice with a little liqueur

The cream:
10 glasses of milk
5 to 6 tbsps of sugar
3 small bags of vanilla corn flour
1 tbsp. of butter, 2 eggs
1 cup of bleached and ground almond

Prepare the "pandespani" mixing all the ingredients and bake it. When cold cut it in 3 parts. Prepare the syrup, the cream and the almonds. Place the three slices of "pandespani" one on top of the other, spreading cream and syrup over each one in turn. Finally sprinkle the ground almonds over the cake.

Efi Varveraki, Heraklion.

Almond roll

(Rolo amigdalou)

150 grams of "filo"(ready-made paper-thin pastry)
150 grams of almonds
100 grams of sugar
150 grams of candied fruit
3 eggs.

The syrup:
1 cup of sugar, 1 cup of water, juice of 1 lemon.

Beat the yolks and mix with the sugar and the beaten whites. Add the almonds and the candied fruit. Butter and spread the "filo" and add the above mixture, close the "filo" forming a roll and bake. After it has cooked, pour syrup over the roll.

Eleni Anemoyanni, Heraklion.

Birthday cake

(Tourta)

8 eggs
1 cup of sugar
vanilla essence
a cup and a half of chopped almonds
a cup and a half of flour

The **syrup:**
2 cups of sugar
2 cups of water

The **cream**:
1 cup of butter
2 cups of caster sugar
half a small cup of coffee (filtered)
2 cups of grated almond

Beat the butter with the sugar and then add the vanilla essence, the almonds and the flour, mixing constantly. Finally add the beaten whites of the eggs and bake the "pandespani". Once it is cold, cut it in 3 slices.

Grapes in syrup

Prepare the syrup: boil the sugar and the water for 5 minutes.

Prepare the cream: beat the butter to a creamy consistence. Little by little add the caster sugar and the coffee, a teaspoonful at a time. Mix.

Bleach the almonds, roast them and grind them.

On each slice of "pandespani", pour one third of the syrup and add one third of the cream; put the slices on top of each other and sprinkle with the almonds.

Ketty Lekka, Heraklion.

Semolina pie

(Galaktoboureko)

1 lb. of "filo"
1 cup of butter
7 glasses of milk
1 cup of fine semolina
1 small bag of vanilla corn flour
vanilla essence
1 and a half cup of sugar
2 tbsps of butter, 4 eggs

The syrup:
3 cups of sugar
2 glasses of water
1 cinnamon stick
the juice of 1 lemon

Prepare the cream with the milk, the semolina and the corn flour. When this is properly mixed, add the beaten eggs, the sugar and the butter.

Butter half the sheets of "filo", place them in a baking tin and spread the cream over them; now butter the second half of the "filo" sheets and place them over the cream. With a knife, lightly mark the serving portions, sprinkle with a little water and bake in a moderate oven until brown.

In the meantime prepare the syrup and when the 'galaktoboureko' is cooked and has cooled, pour the cold syrup over it.

Titika Saklabani, Heraklion.

"Zournadakia"

(Nut-filled filo pastry)

1 kilo walnut
1 kilo of pistachios or almonds
50 grams of sesame seeds
1 cup of sugar
2 tbsps of ground cinnamon
1 kilo of "filo"
a cup and a half of oil

The syrup:
5 cups of sugar
2 glasses of water
the juice of 1 lemon

Mix the sugar with the ground almonds, pistachios, sesame seeds and cinnamon.

Cut every sheet of pastry ("filo") in 4 strips, oil each strip and sprinkle with the above mixture (except for the edges). With a lean stick and beginning at the bottom, twist and wrap the strips, gathering the edges towards the inside of the stick. Pull each strip out of the stick, all wrinkled up, and place it in an oiled tin. Do the same with all the "filo" and all the stuffing.

Before baking in a moderate oven, pour very hot oil on all the rolls. Prepare the syrup; put the rolls in it, bring to the boil and finally drain them.

Titika Miraki, Ayios Myronas

Zournadakia

Small sweet buns with milk cream

(Tsourekakia me anthogala)

1 kilo of milk cream
1 lb. of sugar
4 eggs
1 tbsp. of baking soda
half a small glass of cognac
as much flour as is needed to make a soft dough

Mix the sugar with the cream adding the beaten eggs, the soda dissolved in the cognac and finally the flour. Let the dough stand for half an hour and then shape the buns. Brush them with egg and bake them in a moderate oven.

Fotini Mattheaki, Neapoli.

Easter buns. "Tsourekakia"

Sweet buns with yeast

(Tsourekia me magia)

2 kilos and a half of flour
100 grams of yeast
250 grams of butter
1 cup of oil
750 grams of sugar
6 eggs
1 small bag of baking powder
some vanilla essence
a little salt
1 small bag of ground "machlepi" (a strong sweet smelling spice)
1 small bag of ground mastic
2 glasses of milk

Prepare the leaven on the day before with the yeast, the milk, a little salt and a little flour. Next day add the oil, the butter and the sugar, kneading thoroughly. Then add the beaten eggs, the spices, the baking powder diluted in a little milk and the rest of the flour. Set the dough aside in a warm place and let it rise till it gets to be twice its original size. Finally shape the buns, let them rise again, sprinkle them with ground bleached almonds and bake them.

Anna Katsouloyiorgi, Heraklion.

Easter buns

(Tsourekakia Paschalina)

3 cups of butter
2 and a half cups of sugar
1 glass of milk
3 egg yolks
vanilla essence
1 teasp. of baking soda
3 tbsps of cognac
the juice of 1 lemon
2 kilos of flour

Mix the butter with the sugar. Add the yolks, the vanilla essence, the milk, the soda diluted in the cognac, the lemon and the flour. Shape the buns, brush with a whole egg, a yolk and a little water. Bake.

Ketty Lekka, Heraklion.

«Kataifi»

1 kilo of "kataifi fillo"
1 lb. of roughly ground almonds
2 cups of butter
1 tbsp. and a half of cinnamon
2 tbsps of bread crumbs

the syrup:
1 kilo of sugar
4 glasses of water
vanilla essence
the juice of a lemon

Mix the almonds with the cinnamon and the bread crumbs. Butter a baking tin and spread half the pastry. Add more melted butter and spread the filling. Cover with the other half of the pastry and pour the rest of the melted butter. Bake till golden.

When the "kataifi" has cooled down pour the syrup over it.

Anna Sfakianaki, Heraklion.

"Baklavas"

1 lb. of "filo" (leaf-like pastry)
2 cups of roughly chopped almonds
2 cups of roughly chopped walnuts
2 teasps of ground cinnamon
1 teasp. of ground clove
1 cup of butter

The **syrup:**
3 cups of sugar
2 cups of water
half a cup of honey

2 tbsps of lemon juice
vanilla essence

Mix the walnuts, the almonds and the ground clove and cinnamon. Melt the butter, butter a tin, spread 4 sheets of "filo"; spread a little of the mixture and cover with 2 buttered sheets of the "filo". Continue in this manner till all the ingredients are used up. On top place 4 buttered sheets of the "filo"; now mark the serving portions with a knife, pour the rest of the butter over the sweet and bake in a moderate oven till brown.

In the meantime, prepare the syrup and pour it hot over the hot "baklavas".

Anna Katsoulogiorgi, Heraklion.

Roll of "baklavas"

5 cups of ground walnuts
1 cup of bread crumbs
half a cup of sugar
2 tbsps of ground cinnamon and clove
600 grams of "filo"
1 cup of butter

The syrup:
5 cups of sugar
3 glasses of water
2 tbsps of lemon juice

Mix the walnuts, the bread crumbs, the sugar and the cinnamon and clove. On 2 buttered sheets of "filo" sprinkle some of the mixture; repeat the same operation twice, covering the mixture every time with 1 sheet of thin pastry. Roll up the "filo" with the mixture in the middle and cut up the roll into smaller rolls. Place them upside down in a baking tin, pour the rest of the butter over them and bake.

In the meantime, prepare the syrup and pour it hot on the hot "baklavas".

Buns made with oil

(Koulourakia ladera)

3 cups of oil
2 cups of sugar
2 cups of boiled cinnamon
2 teasps of baking powder
1 teasp. of baking soda
2 kilos of flour (more or less) sesame seeds

Knead the above ingredients in the given order, shape the buns, pour a little liqueur on

Butter and oil buns

them, sprinkle them with some sesame seeds and bake.

Titika Miraki, Ayios Myronas

Buns made with oil and wine

(Koulourakia ladera me krasi)

3cups of oil
2 cups of sugar
1 glass and a half of white wine
half a glass of orange juice
1 and a half teasp. of baking powder
1 and a half teasp. of baking soda
1 tbsp. of ground clove and cinnamon
1 kilo and a half of flour
sesame seeds.

Knead the above ingredients as given above, shape the buns, sprinkle them with sesame and bake them.

Using the same recipe, you can make delicious rusks ("paximadakia").

Titika Miraki, Ayios Myronas

Fried buns

(Koulourakia tiganita)

1 cup of olive-oil
1 cup of sugar
3 eggs
1 teasp. of baking soda
1 teasp. of baking powder
vanilla essence, lemon peel
1 tbsp of ground clove and cinnamon
1 small glass of cognac
3 cups of flour
frying oil
caster sugar

Mix the oil with the butter. Add the yolks one by one and then the beaten whites with the soda disolved in the cognac, the vanilla, the peel and the cinnamon, drawing in the flour bit by bit. Knead into a soft dough.

Shape very small buns and fry them on a moderate flame. Sprinkle them with caster sugar and serve either hot or cold.

Eleni Daouraki, Sitia.

Barley buns

(Koulourakia krithina)

2 cups of oil
2 cups of sugar
1 small glass of raki (alcohol drink)
1 small glass of cognac
1 small glass of boiled cinnamon
1 tbsp. of baking soda
as much barley-flour as you need to make a soft dough

Begin by mixing the oil with the sugar and then add the ingredients in the order given above. Shape the buns and bake them.

Titika Miraki, Ayios Myronas.

Biscuits with coconut

(Biskota me karyda)

1 lb. of butter
1 lb. of sugar
3 eggs
vanilla essence
1 small glass of raki
1 teasp. of baking soda
2 teasps of baking powder
200 grams of ground coconut
1 kilo of flour (more or less)
a little truffle (chocolate)

Mix the sugar with the butter and then add the beaten eggs, the vanilla essence, the soda and the baking powder diluted in the raki, the coconut and the flour. Knead thoroughly and then roll out pieces of the dough, cut out biscuits of different shapes, sprinkle them with truffle and bake in a moderate oven.

Voula Daskalaki, Chania.

Biscuits with jam

Biskota me marmelada)

2 cups of butter
1 cup of sugar
3 eggs
vanilla essence
1 cup of roasted and roughly ground almonds
as much flour as is needed
jam

Mix the butter with the sugar and add the yolks, the vanilla, the almonds, drawing in the flour little by little, kneading constantly. Roll out the dough to a thickness of 1 cm and cut out round pieces. Place them in a buttered tin, brush them with the beaten

Pie with raisins

whites, sprinkle them with the almond and bake. When the pieces are baked and cold, stick them together with any jam you want.

Maria Koundourou, Aghios Nikolaos.

Butter buns

(Koulourakia voutirou)

1 cup of butter
1 cup of sugar
2 yolks
half a cup of milk
orange peel
2 teasps of baking powder
4 cups of flour

Mix the butter with the sugar. Add the rest of the ingredients kneading constantly and then let the dough stand for about an hour. Finally shape the buns, brush them with egg and bake in a moderate oven for 20 minutes.

Titika Saklabani, Heraklion.

«Amigdalota» or almond pasties

1 kilo of blanched and ground almonds
800 grams of caster sugar
8 whites of egg
lemon peel

Mix all the ingredients, having beaten the egg whites first. Shape the almond pasties and bake for about 15 minutes.

Maria Koundourou, Ayios Nicolaos.

Pag. 190:- Rusks with raisins
Pag. 191: - Almond pasties
Pag. 192 - 193: - "Moustacouloura"

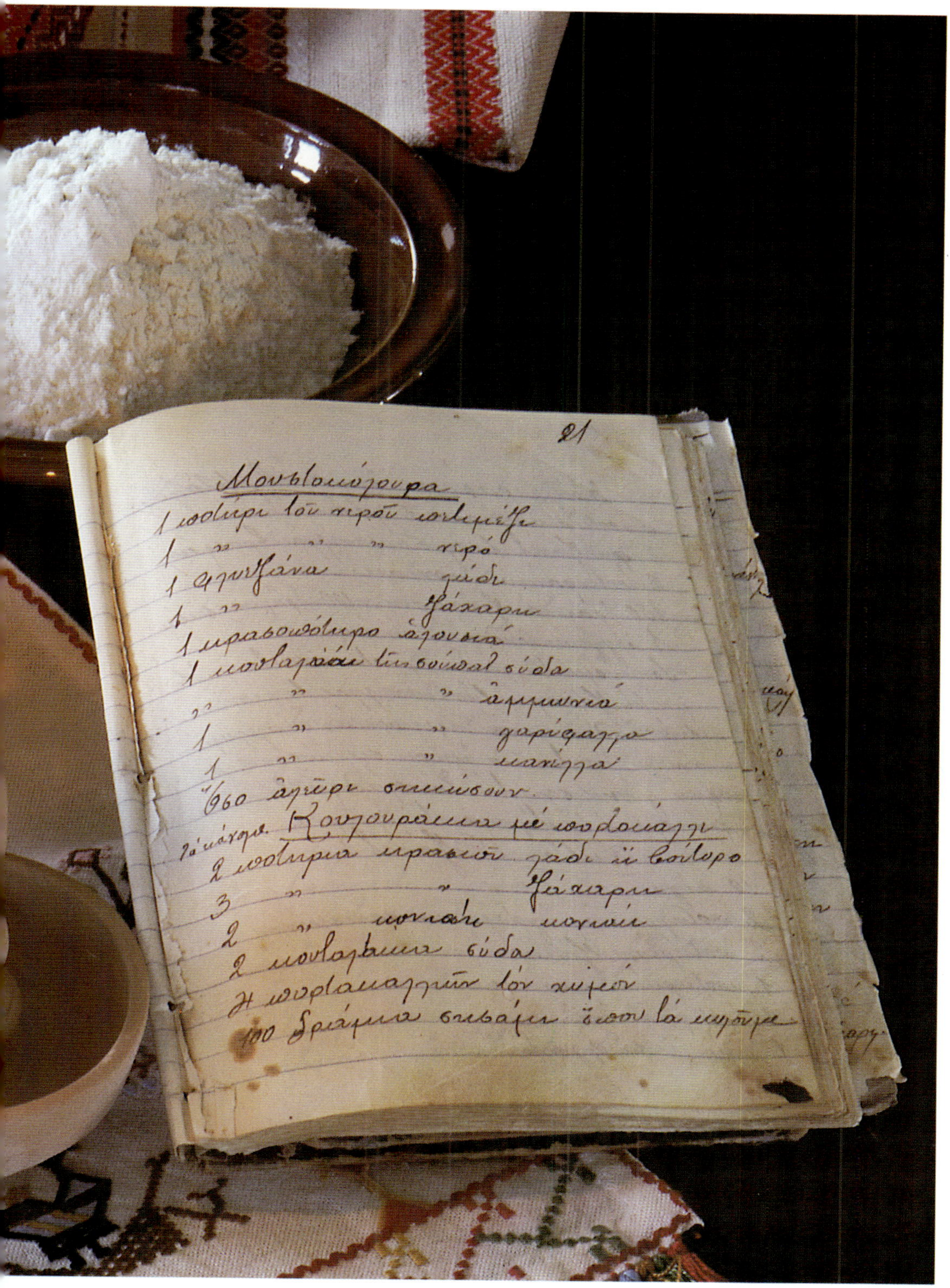

"Moustokouloura" made with white grapes

Buns with must

(Moustokouloura)

2 cups of oil
2 cups of sugar
2 cups of must
3 quarters of a glass of orange juice
2 teasps of baking soda
1 very small glass of cognac
2 teasps of baking powder
2 teasps of ground clove and cinnamon
1 kilo of flour (more or less)
Mix the oil with the sugar and add the must, the soda diluted in the orange juice, the baking powder in the cognac, the clove and cinnamon and the flour. Knead. Shape the buns and bake in a moderate oven.

Titika Saklabani, Heraklion.

Grape-juice syrup

("Petimezi")

Press the juice from fresh grapes and put it in a pot with 2 tbsps of ashes or

"Moustokouloura" with black grapes

pure clay (argil) tied in a clean kitchen towel. Boil the must with the ashes for about 20 to 30 minutes removing the froth formed on the surface of the water. Take the pot from the fire and let it stand for 12 hours. Then sieve the must through a fine cotton cloth, taking care not to upset the sediment; boil this again until it goes brown and turns to a thick syrup.

This grape-juice syrup is used in the preparation of many sweets and pies.

Dried figs with grape-juice syrup

(Sykopitarides me petimezi)

Wash the dried figs, place them in a tin, put 1 tbsp. of grape-juice syrup over each one and bake in a pre-heated oven until the grape-juice syrup sets (about 20 minutes.).

Small apple-pies

These figs ("sykopitarides") can be kept all winter. Put them in layers in a jar with laurel leaves and sesame seeds imbetween.

Amalia Kornarou, Rethimnon.

Buns with grape - juice syrup

(Koulourakia me petimezi)

4 cups of oil
4 cups of grape-juice syrup
2 cups of boiled cinnamon
1 cup of sugar
1 very small glass of raki (alcohol drink)
1 teasp. of ground mastic
the juice and the peel of 1 lemon
2 teasps of baking soda
1 cup of raisins (optional)
flour, as much as you need for a soft dough

Begin by mixing the oil with the sugar and the grape-juice syrup, then add all the other ingredients. Knead, shape the buns and bake in a moderate oven.

Titika Miraki, Ayios Myronas

Must jelly

(Moustalevria)

10 kilos of must that has not been boiled
2 cups of ashes
1 cup of flour (for 5 cups of boiled must)
a handful of roughly chopped walnuts
1 tbsp. of cinnamon
sesame seeds.

Tie the ashes in a clean kitchen towel and put them in the pot with the must; remove the froth which is formed when the must boils. Let it boil for 20 minutes, remove the ashes and let it stand for 12 hours. Then sieve the must through a fine cotton cloth, discarding any ash residue that may have settled on the bottom. Measure out the must (you need 1 cup of flour for 5 of must and put it in a clean pot.

Dilute the flour with some cold must and add this to the boiling must, little by little, stirring constantly. Lower the heat and, always stirring, wait till the must turns to jelly.

Remove the "moustalevria" from the fire and empty it on to several small plates or onto larger ones. Let it cool a bit before sprinkling it with the walnuts, the cinnamon and the sesame seeds.

You can also add some walnuts in the jelly when you are mixing in the diluted flour.

St. Papadaki, Axos, Milopotamos.

Apple pies

(Milopitakia)

the dough:
2 cups of oil
1 small cup of sugar
2 eggs
2 teasps of baking powder
1 small glass of cognac or raki
lemon peel
1 lb. of flour
the filling:
1 kilo yellow apples
4 tbsps of sugar
2 tbsps of ground cinnamon and clove
4 tbsps of raisins
4 tbsps of ground walnuts

Peel and grate the apples and prepare the dough and the filling. Break up the dough into small balls the size of a nut. Roll out these balls and place 1 tbsp. of the filling on one half, cover with the other half, shaping crescents. Bake the apple pies and when they have cooled down, sprinkle with caster sugar and cinnamon

Angeliki Lagouvardou, Heraklion.

- *"Melomakarona"*
- *"Kourabiedes"*
-*"Melomacarona" without syrup*

Honey buns

(Melomakarona)

2 cups of oil
2 cups of sugar
1 cup of boiled cinnamon
1 glass of orange and lemon juice
2 tbsps of baking soda
1 small glass of raki
1 teasp. of baking powder
as much flour as needed

The syrup:
1 glass of honey
1 glass of sugar
1 glass of water
1 stick of cinnamon
sesame seeds and ground cinnamon

Beat the oil and the sugar together and then add the cinnamon, the soda diluted in the fruit juice, the baking powder diluted in the raki and the flour. Knead

Xerotigana

with care and then take pieces of dough the size of a small egg and make them oblong. Bake the "melomakarona" in a moderate oven.

While they are cooling, clean and roast the sesame seeds, mix them with a teasp. of cinnamon in order to sprinkle the melomakarona later and prepare the syrup. While the syrup is boiling on a low flame, dip the melomakarona in for 1 minute, take them out on to a plate and sprinkle with the mixture of the sesame seeds and the cinnamon.

+Eleni Anemoyanni, Heraklion.

«Melamakarona» with walnuts

4 cups of oil
2 cups of sugar
half a glass of water
1 tbsp. of honey
1 glass of orange juice
1 teasp. of baking powder
1 teasp. of baking soda
1 teasp. of orange peel
1 tbsp. of ground clove and cinnamon
1 cup of roughly ground walnuts
as much flour as needed for a soft dough.

The syrup:
1 glass of water
2 cups of sugar
1 cup of honey

roughly ground walnuts and cinnamon for sprinkling the "melomakarona" which you prepare according to the previous recipe. The walnuts are added to the dough with the other ingredients.

Efi Varveraki, Heraklion

Christmas biscuits

Biskota christougeniatika)

1 kilo of flour
2 cups of honey
3 cups of sugar
200 grams of ground almonds
150 grams of candied fruit
the peel of 3 oranges
2 tbsps of cinnamon
2 tbsps of clove
2 tbsps of baking powder
2 eggs
2 tbsps of butter

Mix the flour, the sugar, the cinnamon and clove, the orange peel and the baking powder. Make a hole in the middle and add the honey, the beaten eggs, the butter and the ground and slightly roasted almonds. Knead and let the dough stand for half an hour. Roll out the dough into a thin paste (the thickness of a coin) and cut out the biscuits in any shape you like. Bake for ten minutes in a moderate oven.

Anna Katsouloyiorgi, Heraklion.

«Patouda»

The dough:
5 cups of oil
3 cups of "alousia" or water
1 glass of orange juice
1 small glass of raki
1 teasp. of baking soda
as much flour as needed

The stuffing:
1280 grams of ground walnuts and almonds
600 grams honey and a cup of sugar
1 glass of water
grated orange peel

Patouda

4 tbsps of oil
1 tbsp. of ground nutmeg and 1 tbsp. of ground clove and cinnamon
4 tbsps of crumbled rusk
Prepare the dough and the filling.

Separate the dough into small balls the size of a mandarine. Roll out these balls and place 1 tbsp. of the filling on one half of each and cover with the other half to form crescents. Bake the "patouda" and when they have cooled down, sprinkle with caster sugar.

Maria Fotinaki, Ierapetra.

Stuffed buns

(Koulourakia patoudera)

The stuffing:
3 oranges boiled in their peel and mashed
300 grams of sugar
1 glass of honey
3 cups of bread-or rusk-crumbs
3 cups of bleached and ground almonds
1 teasp. of cinnamon

The dough:
2 cups of butter
2 cups of milk cream
2 cups of sugar
1 glass of warm water or "alousia"
less than a kilo of flour

Mix the ingredients for the stuffing. Prepare the dough mixing the ingredients in the given order. Now take some dough, the size of a walnut and in the middle open a hole to put in a little of the stuffing. Rub the dough so as to get the stuffing ("patoudo") to spread inside and shape the buns. You can prick them with a pin, if you like. Bake in a moderate oven.

Titika Miraki,
Ayios Myronas.

Buns with raisins

(Stafidota)

The dough:
4 cups of oil
1 and a half cup of sugar
1 glass of orange juice
1 small glass of raki
vanilla essence
2 teasps of baking powder
1 teasp. of baking soda
as much flour as is needed for a soft dough

The stuffing:
1 kilo of raisins
3 cups of ground walnuts and almonds
2 tbsps of oil
1 teasp. of lemon peel
2 tbsps of ground clove and cinnamon
Proceed as for the above recipe, but in the end you can dip them, for 1-2 minutes, in syrup made with 1 glass of sugar, 1 glass of honey and 1 glass of water.

Maria Fotinaki, Ierapetra.

Small rusks with almonds

(Paximadakia me amygdala)

5 cups of oil
5 cups of sugar
3 cups of roasted and roughly ground almonds or walnuts
1 glass of orange juice
1 small glass of cognac
1 teasp. of orange peel
1 glass of warm water
1 teasp. of baking soda
4 teasps of baking powder
2 teasps of cinnamon
a bit over 2 kilos of flour
Heat the oil and stir while you add the

Buns with raisins

Cretan peasant

sugar, the almonds, the water, the soda diluted in the orange juice, the baking powder diluted in the cognac and the flour. Knead thoroughly and then shape small loaves. Cut the surface into slices (but not all the way down: the loaf has to remain whole) and bake for about half an hour. Now break away each slice and bake again in a warm oven (100 degrees Celsius).

Titika Miraki, Ayios Myronas.

Chocolate truffles with chestnuts

(Troufes me kastana)

700 grams of cleaned and boiled chestnuts
800 grams of butter
1 cup of caster sugar
2 cups of ground walnut
250 grams of cooking chocolate
1 small glass of liqueur
250 grams of chocolate truffle

Boil and mince the chestnuts. Add the melted butter, the melted chocolate and the sugar. Stir while adding the liqueur and the walnuts; let the mixture cool down. Then shape little balls with the mixture, roll them in the chocolate truffle and place each ball in a special little truffle paper.

"Fanouropita"

This is the cake made in honour of Ayios Fanourios on his nameday on the 27th of August: this Saint is particularly venerated in Crete, although some have doubted he ever existed and he's not mentioned in any of the Lives of the Saints. Many Cretans, on the other hand, believe that Ayios Fanourios can find lost objects, animals and even people if one invokes his help. Then, in an act of thanksgiving, a special cake ("fanouropita") is made and taken to church where it is given out to the faithful after mass. On the 27th of August at dawn one can see dozens of these cakes in many Cretan churches, especially those dedicated to the Saint: every housewife has seen to it that her cake is at least as savoury and as beautiful as the next one. Recipes of this cake are to be found in the 19th century notebooks on cookery that we still have, a proof that this custom is not a recent one.

Ingredients:
1 cup of oil
2 cups of sugar
1 cup of orange juice
half a cup of raki or cognac
1 cup of walnuts
1 cup of apple or other fruit
1 tbsp. of ground cinnamon and clove
1 tbsp. of baking powder
1 cup of raisins
as much flour as needed (about half a kilo)

Begin mixing the oil and the sugar, then add the cognac, the baking powder dissolved in the orange juice, the cinnamon and clove, the raisins, the fruit, the walnuts and finally the flour. Work the mixture until all the ingredients have amalgamated and pour it in an oiled baking tin: sprinkle with sesame seeds and bake for about one hour.

Eleni Simitzi, Rethimnon.

Saint Fanourios' cake

Almond cakes:

(Kourabiedes)

700 grams of butter
300 grams of olive-oil
1 cup of caster sugar
3 yolks and 1 white
1 teasp. of baking soda
1 very small glass of cognac
1 tbsp. and a half of cinnamon
700 grams of bleached and roughly ground almonds in their skins
as much flour as needed
1 lb of caster sugar

Mix the butter and the oil with the sugar and add the beaten eggs, the soda diluted in the cognac, the cinnamon and the almonds. Knead thoroughly and then take pieces of dough the size of a walnut and give them either a round or an oblong shape. Bake the kourabiedes for 20 minutes. When they are cold, sprinkle with caster sugar.

Ketty Lekka, Heraklion.

«Kourabiedes» with syrup

1 cup of sugar, 1 glass of water
1 lb. of butter, 3 yolks
1 tbsp. of baking soda
the juice of half a lemon
flour or semolina

The **syrup:**
4 cups of sugar
2 glasses of water

Prepare the syrup boiling 1 cup of sugar in 1 glass of water for 5 minutes. When it is just warm, beat the butter till it goes white and little by little add the syrup, the yolks, the baking soda dissolved in the lemon juice and the flour. Knead. Then shape the kourabiedes and bake them. When they are just warm, carefully pour the syrup over them with a spoon.

Efi Varveraki, Heraklion.

«Chalvas»

3 cups of oil
1 cup of rough semolina and 2 of fine semolina
1 handful of walnuts and one of pine kernels
1 tbsp. of ground clove and cinnamon

The syrup:
2 cups of sugar
3 cups and a half of water
1/2 cup of orange syrup
1/2 cup of candied fruit
orange and 2 of bitter orange
a handful of raisins
1 stick of cinnamon

Heat the oil in a saucepan with the orange peel; now remove the orange peel and add the semolina, the ground cinnamon and clove, the roughly ground walnuts and the pine kernels, stirring constantly. Brown the semolina and then add the syrup which you have prepared in another saucepan in the meantime; stir vigorously.

The "halvas" can be served in a large mould or in several small ones.

Efi Varveraki, Heraklion.

Baked «chalvas»

1 cup of butter
2 cups of sugar
2 cups of yoghurt
3 eggs
3 cups of semolina
1 tbsp. of baking soda
2 tbsps. of cognac
1 cup of roughly ground walnuts or almonds
1 tbsp. of cinnamon

The **syrup**:
2 cups of sugar
2 cups of water
1 stick of cinnamon

Mix the butter, the sugar and the yoghurt. Add the beaten yolks, the semolina, the soda dissolved in the

"Sykopitaridés"

cognac, the cinnamon, the walnuts or the almonds and the beaten whites. Pour the mixture into a buttered tin and bake in a moderate oven.

After you have taken the "chalvas" out of the oven, pour the hot syrup over it, which you have prepared in the meantime.

+Eleni Anemoyanni, Heraklion.

Fritters

(Xerotigana)

1 kilo of flour
1 small glass of raki
1 tbsp. of oil
a little salt
as much water as needed (about 2 glasses).

The syrup:
2 cups of sugar
1 glass of water
cinnamon
5 or 6 tbsps of honey
half a small glass of lemon juice
cinnamon and ground nuts for the sprinkling

Knead a rather stiff dough with the above ingredients. Roll out the paste to a long thin ribbon (1 meter) and then cut it in 4.

Heat the oil in a pan. Wrap each ribbon separately around your fingers, first using two, then three and then four; stick the edge and deep-fry. With the help of two forks, turn these rings upside down, taking care not to spoil the shape. When each fritter is nice and brown, take it out of the pan and place it on kitchen paper.

Prepare the syrup when all the fritters are ready. Boil the sugar in water, with the cinnamon, for 15 minutes and then add the honey and the lemon. Dip each fritter in the very hot syrup and when you take it out, place it on a dish and sprinkle with the nuts (or sesame seeds) and the cinnamon.

Adrianna Markoutsaki, Kapsodasos, Sfakia.

«Avgokalamara»

5 eggs
5 tbsps of oil
5 tbsps of sugar
5 tbsps of raki
1 glass of milk
1 small bag of baking powder
The syrup: 3 cups of sugar
1 glass of water
cinnamon, ground walnuts and sesame seeds for the sprinkling

Mix the oil with the sugar, the raki, the milk and the baking powder. Little by little draw in the flour and knead thoroughly.

Roll out the dough to a thickness of half a centimetre and cut out pieces of 10 cms by 10cms which you wrap in the shape of cones with the help of two forks; these you deep-fry. Then place them on absorbing kitchen paper and prepare the syrup. Finally, dip each "cone" or "avgokalamaro" in the boiling syrup, place it on a plate and sprinkle with walnuts or sesame seeds and cinnamon.

Evgenia Katsanevaki, Askyfou, Sfakia.

Beignets or «Svingi»

2 cups of water
2 cups of flour
1 cup of butter
6 eggs
1 teasp. of salt
2 teasps of baking soda
2 cinnamon sticks, lemon peel

Bring to the boil the water, the soda, the butter, the cinnamon and the lemon peel. Add the flour and stir vigorously with a wooden spoon until the paste leaves the sides of the pan. Draw away from the fire and rest for a few minutes. Then add the eggs one by one, stirring vigorously.

Have ready a deep pan with oil and when very hot, take a teasp. of the paste and drop into the pan one at a time, taking care to dip the spoon every time into cold water to keep the

Beignets simples

paste from sticking on to it. When the "svingi" are golden, take them out of the oil and sprinkle with caster sugar mixed with cinnamon.

You can also serve them with the following **syrup**: boil 2 cups of sugar, 1 cup of water, 2 or 3 tbsps. of honey, a cinnamon stick and some lemon peel for 10 minutes; remove the spices and add a small glass of cognac.

Anna Katsouloyiorgi, Heraklion.

Plain fritters

(Tiganites)

2 or 3 glasses of water
1 tbsp. of oil
1 tbsp. of lemon juice
1 teasp. of salt
1 lb. of flour
honey or grape-juice syrup
sesame seeds and ground walnuts

Put the flour in a bowl, open a hole in the middle and put in the oil, the lemon juice and the salt. Mix, add water and keep on stirring vigorously until you obtain a batter. Have ready a deep pan with oil and when it is hot, take tbsps of batter and drop them in the oil one at a time: when the fritters are golden, place them in a plate, pour some honey or grape-juice syrup and sprinkle sesame seeds and the ground walnuts over them.

Chrys. Pattakou, Ayia Paraskevi, Amari.